Geo. H. Heffner.

THE

YOUTHFUL WANDERER;

OR

AN ACCOUNT OF A TOUR THROUGH ENGLAND, FRANCE, BELGIUM, HOLLAND, GERMANY AND THE RHINE, SWITZERLAND, ITALY, AND EGYPT,

ADAPTED TO THE WANTS OF YOUNG AMERICANS TAKING THEIR FIRST GLIMPSES AT THE OLD WORLD.

BY

GEO. H. HEFFNER.

OREFIELD:
A. S. HEFFNER, PRINTER.
1876.

PREFACE.

It had been fashionable among the ancients, for men of learning to visit distant countries and improve their education by traveling, after they had completed their various courses of study in literary institutions, and the same custom still prevails in Europe at the present time; but in our country, comparatively few avail themselves of this finishing course. It is not strange that this should have been so with a people who are separated from the rest of the world by such wide oceans as we are, which could, up to a comparatively recent period, only have been crossed at a sacrifice of much time and money, and at the risk of loosing either life or health. These difficulties have been greatly reduced by the application of steam-power to navigation, and the time has come when an American can make the tour of Europe with but little more expenditure of time and money than it costs even a native of Europe to do it.

One of my principal objects in writing this book is to encourage others to make similar tours. We would have plenty of books no traveling, if some of them did represent the readers in the humbler spheres of life, but the general impression in America is that no one can see Europe to any satisfaction in less than a year or two and with an outlay of from a thousand to two thousand dollars. This is a great mistake. If one travels for pleasure mainly, it will certainly require a great deal of time and money, but a hard-working student can do much in a few months. Permit me to say, that one will see and experience more in two weeks abroad, than many a learned man in America expects could be seen in a year. I sometimes give the particulars of sights and adventures in detail, that the reader may take an example of my experience, for any tour he may propose to make. The times devoted to different places are given that he may form an estimate of the comparative importance of different places.

Statistics form a leading feature of this work, and these have been gathered and compiled with special reference to the wants of the student. Many an American scholar studies the geography and history of foreign countries at a great disadvantage, because he can not obtain a general idea of the institutions of Europe, unless he reads half a dozen works on the subject. To do this he has not the time. This work gives, in the compass of a single volume, a general idea of all the most striking features of the manners, customs and institutions of the people of some eight different nations speaking as many different languages and dialects.

As the sights that one sees abroad are so radically different from what we are accustomed to see at home, I feel pained whenever I think of describing them to any one. If you would know the nature of my perplexity, then go to Washington and see the stately magnificence of our National Capitol there, and then go and describe what you have seen to one who has never seen a larger building than his village church; or go and see the Centennial Exposition at Philadelphia, and then tell your neighbor who has never seen anything greater than a county fair, how, what he has seen compares with the World's Fair! I too am proud of our country, (not so much for what she now is, but because she promises to become the greatest nation that ever existed), but it must be confessed, that America presents little in the sphere of architecture that bears comparison with the castles, palaces and churches of the Old World. The Capitol at Washington, erected at the cost of twelve and a half millions, the City Hall of Baltimore, perhaps more beautiful but less magnificent, and other edifices that have been erected of late, are structures of which we may justly be proud; but let us take the buildings of the "Centennial Exposition" for a standard and compare them with some of those in Europe. The total expenses incurred in erecting all the exposition buildings, and preparing the grounds, &c., with all the contingent expenses, is less than ten million. But St. Peter's in Rome cost nine times, and the palace and pleasure-garden of Versailles twenty times as much as this! It is safe to assert, that if a young man had but two hundred dollars with six weeks of time at his command, and would spend it in seeing London and Paris, he could never feel sorry for it. *Young student go east.*

CONTENTS.

CHAPTER I.

CHAPTER II.

CHAPTER III.

PAGE.

CHAPTER VII.

LONDON TO PARIS.

CHAPTER VIII.

PARIS.

CHAPTER XIII.

CHAPTER XIV.

THE PALATINATE, (*Die Pfalz*).

CHAPTER XV.

SWITZERLAND.

☞ Subjects treated in a general way are distinguished by being rendered in italics, in this table of contents.

THE KEYSTONE STATE NORMAL SCHOOL.

CHAPTER I.

LEAVING HOME.

While engaged in making the preliminary arrangements for leaving soon after the "Commencement" of the Keystone State Normal School (coming off June 24th), information was received that the "Manhattan," an old and well-tried steamer of the Guion Line, would sail from New York for Liverpool on the 22nd of June. She had been upon the ocean for nine years, and had acquired the reputation of being "*safe but slow.*" As I esteemed *life* more precious than *time*, though either of them once lost can never be recovered, I soon decided to share my fate with her—by her, to be carried safely to the "farther shore," or with her, to seek a watery grave.

The idea of remaining for the Commencement, was at once abandoned; short visits, abrupt farewells, and a hasty preparation for the pilgrimage, were my portion for the few days still left me, and Saturday, the 19th, was determined upon as the day for leaving home. It would be evidence of gross ingratitude to forget the kind wishes, tender good-byes, and many other marks of attention, on the part of friends and acquaintances, which characterized the parting hour. Both Literary Societies had passd resolutions to turn out, and on the ringing of the bell at 6:30 a. m., all assembled in the Chapel, and addresses were delivered.

Half an hour later, we left in procession for the depot, where we arrived in time to exchange our last tokens of remembrance—cards, books, bouquets &c., and shake hands once more.

While the train was moving away, the benedictions and cheers of a hundred familiar voices rang upon the air, and waving handkerchiefs caught the echoes even from the distant cupola of the now fast receding Normal School buildings. A number of torpedoes that had been placed under the wheels of the locomotive, had already apprised us that the train was in motion, and would soon hurry us out of sight. During all this excitement of the parting hour, which seemed to affect some so deeply, I was either looking into the future, or contemplating the present, rather, from an *active* than from a *passive* stand-point; and, as a natural consequence, remained quite tranquil and composed--my feelings and emotions being at a lower ebb than they could now be, if the occasion would repeat itself. The idea of making a tour through Europe and to the Orient, had been continually revolving in my mind for many years; and now, that I saw the prospect open of once realizing the happy dreams of my childhood, and the schemes of early youth, I took no time for contemplating the dangers of sea voyages or any of the other perils of adventure.

Before we came to Easton, I formed the acquaintance of a Swiss mother, who seemed much pleased to find one that was about to visit her dear "Fatherland," where she had spent the sunny days of her childhood. After giving me directions and letters of introduction, she entreated me very earnestly to visit her home and kin, and bring them word from her.

New York was reached at 12:10 p. m. As there were but three days remaining for seeing the city, I immediately began my visits to some of its principal points of interest. Having first engaged a room at a hotel in the vicinity of the new Post-Office, I commenced to stroll about, and at 5:30 p. m., entered Trinity Church. Its capacious interior soon disclosed to me numerous architectural peculiarities, such as are characteristic of the English parish churches or of cathedrals in general; and which render old Trinity quite conspicuous among her American sisters. A fee of twelve cents entitled me to an ascent of its lofty spire, which can be made to the height of 304 (?) steps, or about 225 feet.

Sunday, June 20th. Rose at 4:30 a. m. and visited Central Park. This being an importune time for seeing the gay and fashionable life of the city, I contended myself with a walk to the Managerie, and returned in time to attend the forenoon service of Plymouth Church, in Brooklyn. I reached the place before 9:00 o'clock, and formed the acquaintance of a young gentleman who was a great admirer of the Rev. Henry Ward Beecher, and, being an occasional visitor at this church, knew how to get a seat in that congregation, which generally closed its doors against the faces of hundreds, after every available seat was occupied. We at once took our stand at the middle gate, and there endured the pressure of the crowd for more than half an hour before the doors opened. We were the first two that entered, and running up stairs at the head of the dashing throng, succeeded in making sure of a place in the audience. The church has seating capacity for about 2,800 adults. All the pews are rented to members of the congregation by the year, except the outer row of seats along the three walls; but these are generally all occupied in one or several minutes after the doors open.

The choir files in at 10:25. A "voluntary" by the organist at 10:30, and by the choir at 10:32, during which time Mr. Beecher comes in, jerks his hat behind a boquet stand, and takes his seat. Leads in a prayer in so low a strain that he can not be understood at any remote place in the audience. At 10:55 he baptizes eight infants, whose names are passed to him on cards. Concludes another prayer at 11:20 and aunounces his text, "Christ and bim crucified." 1 Cor. II. 2

EXTRACTS FROM THE SERMON.

"One of Christ's followers once said, 'If all that

Christ said and did were written in books, the world could not contain them.' This is an *exageration*, (*a ripple of laughter dances over the congregation*), having a great meaning, however." * * * * "David gives us only his *intense* life." (*The audience smile*). (11:35). The preacher becoming dramatic in gesticulation and oratorical in delivery, walks back and forth upon the elevated platform. While describing the crosses which he saw yesterday, he becomes highly excited, swinging his arms above his head. "Crosses everywhere. All the way up street; on every beauty's breast." (*Explosive laughter*). "Some may have cost $500, others possibly $1,500; perhaps some cost $2,000." (*Claps his hands in excitement*). * * * * "Some say 'the church handed down Christianity'; but I say Christianity kept the church alive. What was it, that, in the Reformation, made blood such a sweet manure for souls?" (12:10 p. m.) Pleads earnestly for the weak and the erring. "A man that has gone wrong, and has nobody to be sorry for it, is lost; pity may save." Sermon concluded at 12:25. Prayer. Dismissal by singing.

Mr. Beecher's voice is so clear and powerful, that he can be readily understood in the most distant parts of the house. After leaving church, I went up to Columbia Heights, the most aristocratic section of Brooklyn, where I enjoyed myself in contemplating the beautiful and magnificent buildings which constitute the quiet and charming homes of those wealthy people living there. How partial Heaven is to some of her children! Thence I found my way to Greenwood Cemetery, where I spent the remainder of the day amid the tombs and monuments of "the great city of the dead." Guide books containing all the carriage roads and foot-paths of that burial ground, are sold at or near the gate. One of these I procured, and found it was so perfect in the particulars, that I could readily find the grave of any one of the many distinguished persons mentioned in the index, without further assistance whatever. It is impossible here to give an account of the many splendid tombs and monuments erected there by loving hearts and skillful hands, in memory of dear friends and relatives that have "gone away!" What multitudes of strange and curious designs meet the eye here! Some few perhaps seem odd; but most of them bear appropriate emblems, and convey sweet thoughts and tender sentiments in behalf of those "sleeping beneath the sod." What a place for meditation! How quiet, how solemn! No one should visit New York without allotting at least half a day to these holy grounds. How I wander from grave to grave! Here I am struck with the text of an impressive epitaph, and there I see the delicate and elaborate workmanship of a skillful master. Here my heart is touched by the sweet simplicity of a simple slab bearing some touching lines, there I stand in silent admiration before the magnificent proportions of a towering monument, or sit down to study the meaning of some obscure design. A mere sketch of all that I saw there would fill a volume, but I found one monument which I cannot pass by without some notice. It stands on Hilly Ridge, and was erected to the memory of six "*lost at sea*, on board the steamer "Arctic," Sept. 27th, 1854." These words arrested my attention, and a minute later, I had ascended the domical summit of the hill, and stood at the foot of the high monument. It has a square granite base upon which stand four little red pillars of polished Russian granite, supporting a transversely arched canopy, with a high spire. Under the canopy is represented the Ocean and the shipwreck of the "Arctic." The vessel is assailed by a terrible storm, and fiercely tossed upon the foaming waves! She has already sprung a leak, and through the ugly gash admits a copious stream of the fatal liquid, while the raging sea, like an angry monster, is about to swallow her distined prey! Down she goes, and among the many passengers on board, are

GRACE,

wife of Geo. F. Allen and daughter of James Brown,
born Aug. 25th, 1821.

HERBERT,

infant child of Geo. F. and Grace Allen,
born Sept. 28th, 1853.

WILLIAM B.,
son of James Brown,
born April 23rd, 1825.

CLARA,
wife of Wm. B. Brown and daughter of Chas. Moulton,
born June 30th, 1830.

CLARA ALICE JANE,
daughter of William B. and Clara Brown,
born Aug. 30th, 1852.

MARIA MILLER,
daughter of James Brown,
born Sept. 30th, 1833.

What a sad story! As the shipwreck occurred in the fall, it is highly probable that the party was homeward bound, and, had better fortune been with them, might in a very few days have again been safe and happy in their respective homes, relating stories of their strange but pleasant experiences in the Old World. How changed the tale! How their friends must have been looking and waiting for the "Arctic!" One line told the whole story, and perhaps all that was ever heard of them, "The "Arctic" is wrecked!"

Not far away, on the crown of Locust Hill, sleeps Horace Greeley, America's great journalist and political economist. At the head of his grave stands a temporal memorial stone in the form of a simple marble slab, bearing the inscription, "Horace Greeley, born February 3rd, 1811; died November 29th, 1872." I left the Cemetery at

7:45 p. m., and returned to my quarters in New York.

Monday, June 21st. Having procured passage with the "Manhattan," which was to sail on the morrow, I straightway went to Pier No. 46, North River, *to take a look at her!* At 12:45 p. m. I stood in the third story of A. T. Stewart's great dry goods establishment, perhaps the largest of the kind in the world. It is six stories high, and covers nearly two acres of ground. My next point of destination was Brooklyn Court-House. The afternoon session opened at 2:00 o'clock, but I did not reach the place until half an hour later. The court-room was crowded as usual, and many had been turned away, who stood in knots about the halls and portico, holding the posts, and discussing politics and church matters. I entered hastily, like one behind time and in a hurry, and inquired where the court-room was. "It is crowded to overflowing, you can not enter," was the reply; but I went for the reporter's door. A few raps, and it was opened. I offered my card and asked for a place in the audience as a reporter. The reply was that the room was already jammed full. But I retained my position in the door all the same! "What paper do you represent?" asked the door-keeper. "I am a correspondent of the *National Educator*" was my response; whereupon he bid me step in. The court-room was a small one for the occasion, affording seats for about 400 on the floor, and for 125 more in the gallery. Some twenty-five or thirty ladies were scattered through the audience. Mr. Beech, Tilton's senior lawyer, was summing up his closing speech. Tilton and Fullerton sat immediately behind him, but Mr. Beecher was not in court. Toward the close of the session there was a kind of "clash of arms" among the opposing lawyers. Fullerton repeated the challenge previously made by Beech, offering to prove that corrupt influences were made to bear upon the jury. The Judge appointed a time for hearing the complaint, and adjourned the Court.

BARNUM'S HIPPODROME

was visited in the evening, where I saw for the first time on a grand scale, the charming features of the European "*cafe*" (pronounced cä'fā'). Here are combined the attractions of the pleasure garden or public square, with the ornaments and graces of the ball-room and the opera. It is a magnificent parlor abounding in trees, fountains, statuary and rustic retreats. Gilmore's large band of seventy-five to a hundred pieces, occupying an elevated platform in the centre, render excellent music. Fifteen hundred to two thousand gas jets, eveloped by globes of different colors (red, white, blue, yellow and green) and blazing from the curves of immense arches, spanning the Hippodrome in different directions, illuminate the entire building with the brilliancy of the noon-day sun. To the right of the entrance is an artificial water-fall about thirty feet in height. Two stationary engines supply the water, elevating 1,800 gallons per minute, which issues from beneath the arched roof of a subterranean cavern, and dashing down in broken sheets over a series of cascades and rapids, plunges into a basin below. From this basin it flows away into tanks in an other building, where four to five tons of ice are consumed daily to keep it at a low temperature, so that the vapor and breeze produced by this ice-water, at the foot of the cataract, refreshes the air and keeps it cool and pleasant during the warm summer evenings. The admittance is fifty cents, and 5,000 to 10,000 persons enter every night, during the height of the season. Here meets "youth and beauty," and the wealth, gayety and fashion of New York is well represented.

Tuesday, June 22d. I spent the morning in writing farewell letters, and making the final preparations for leaving. At one o'clock I went on board the "Manhattan," which was still quite empty. In order to have something to do by which to while away the slow dull hours yet remaining, I commenced writing a letter. None of my friends or acquaintances being with me, I bid all my farewells by note. But such writing! Though the vessel was locked to the pier by immense cables, still she was anything but steady. As passengers began to multiply, acquaintances were formed. By and by the stewart came around, and assigned to us our berths. Ship government is monarchic in form. The officers have almost absolute authority, and the passengers, like bashful pupils, do their best to learn the new rules and regulations and adapt their conduct to them, as soon as possible, so that nobody may find occasion for making observations or passing remarks. All these things remind one very much of a first day at school. As

THE PARTING HOUR

approaches, large numbers of the friends and relatives of some of our passengers, came upon deck to bid good-by. Some cried, others laughed, and many more *tried* to laugh. Some that seemed to relish repetition, or were carried away by enthusiasm and the excitement of the hour, shook hands over and over again with the same person. At 3:00 o'clock p. m., the gangway was lowered and the cables were removed. A shock, a boom, and the vessel swung away and glided into the river! The die was cast, and our fate was sealed. Shouts and huzzas rent the air, as the steamer skimmed proudly over the waves, while clouds of handkerchiefs, on deck and upon the receding shore, waved in the air as long as we could see each other. Down, down the river glided the steady "Manhattan," and our thoughts began to run in new channels. "Good-by! dear, sweet America," thought we a hundred times, while we watched the retreating shores; perhaps our thoughts were whispers! Europe with its innumerable attractions, its Alps, Appennines and Vesuvius, its castles, palaces, walled towns, fine cities, great battle fields, ancient ruins and a thousand other milestones of civilization, lay before us; but a wide Ocean, and all the dangers and perils of a long sea voyage lay between us and that other—longed for shore.

The question whether we would ever realize the pleasure of a visit to the Old World, was now reduced to the alternatives of *success*, or *failure by accident or disease.*

SEA-SICKNESS.

I had labored under the erroneous impression that sea-sickness was bred of fear and terror, and would attack only women (of both sexes) and children of tender minds and frail constitutions. But, when the waves commenced to roll higher, and the ship began a ceaseless rocking, which was in direct opposition to the wants and comfort of my system, as all manner of swinging ever was, I began to have fears that it was not *fright*, but *swinging*, that made people sick at sea. The inner man threatened to rebel, and I made my calculations how much higher the billows might swell, before stomachs would be apt to revolt. We sailed out of sight of the land before dusk, by which time, however, numbers of ill-mannered stomachs had given evidence of their bad humor. Though I nodded but once or twice to old Neptune, during the entire voyage, still I suffered much during the first five days, from the pressure of intense dizziness and headache, occasioned by the incessant rocking of our vessel upon the restless waves. We had a very fine passage, as the sailors would say, but it was far from being as fine as I had always fancied fine sea voyages would be. The rocking of the ship would never be less than about two feet up and down in its width of thirty feet. When the winds blew hard and the waves rolled high, it swung some twenty or twenty-five feet up and down at its bow and at the stern. The highest waves that we saw in our outward passage were probably from twelve to eighteen feet. That the rocking or swinging of the ship, is the one and only cause of sea-sickness, may admit of a question; but that it is the principal cause, there can be little doubt. My observations and experiences in five or six voyages (long and short) did not point to any other cause. As the sea air is generally regarded as more salubrious and healthier than that on land, it can certainly not be a cause of sea-sickness. Fright and terror, in a timid person might perhaps aggravate the disease in few instances, though it seems doubtful, to say the least. When the sea is calm and smooth, everybody feels well, even if the vessel swims in the middle of the Ocean; but let a storm come on, and the number of sick will increase in proportion to its violence.

WHALES.

On the second day of our voyage, in the afternoon at about 4:00 o'clock, we came across a shoal of whales. There must have been two or three dozen of them. They apparently avoided our ship, as only a few made their appearance very close by, though we sailed through the midst of them. They swam about leisurely near the surface, betraying their whereabouts frequently by spouting; but occasionally they would rise considerably above the surface of the water, and expose large portions of their bodies to our view. The excitement occasioned among all on board, by the appearance of so many of these terrible monsters, greatly quickened our dull spirits, and tended much to alleviate the lonesomeness occasioned by the monotony of the sea voyage.

No one who has never experienced it, can form an idea of how the mind is depressed and benumbed by the monotony of sea life. The nights drag along *so* slowly, and the days—they seem to have no end. One will often loose his "bearings" so completely, that he knows neither what day of the week it is, nor whether it is forenoon or afternoon. Without keeping a diary or record of some kind, it would be difficult for many to keep a sure run of the date. Ordinarily, one sits down early in the morning *to wait for the evening to draw by*, and often it happens, when it seems to him that he has waited the length of three days on the land, he is mortified by the announcement that it is yet far from being noon! An eternal present seems to swallow up both the past and the future. After a week or two of such weary waiting, one feels as if he had forgotten almost every thing that happened before the day of his leaving home. I remarked one day to a company of passengers on deck, that I could scarcely recall any thing that had happened in the past; indeed, it required quite an effort to remember that I had ever been in America, or anywhere else except on the old "Manhattan" in an everlasting voyage. "Yes," observed one of the company, "and I heard a fellow say yesterday that time seemed so long to him, that he had really forgotten how many children he had." There is little doubt, that if a ship-load of passengers could be suddenly and unexpectedly landed upon the grassy slope of a verdant hill-side; many would under the momentary impulse of overwhelming pleasure, kiss the dear earth, as Columbus did on landing at San Salvador, if, indeed, extreme joy did not impel them to make themselves ridiculous by imitating old Nebuchadnezzar, in commmencing to graze on the herbage! But the longest day must have an end, and so have sea voyages.

THE FIRST SIGHT OF LAND.

On Saturday morning, July 3rd, everybody came upon deck in hope of seeing land. A report was soon circulated, that the sailors with their telescopes, had already seen the mountains of Ireland. Those passengers that had telescopes or opera glasses soon brought them upon deck. Some said they saw the land, but others using the same glasses could see nothing. This created a pleasant excitement with but little satisfaction, however, except a lively hope of soon seeing *terra firma* again. At about 8:00 o'clock (4:00 o'clock Penna. time) it was believed by the passengers generally, that land was really in sight. When I first saw the outline of the mountains through the mist and clouds that hung near the horizon, it stood out so clear and bold that I felt surprised at not having been able to see it long before, as some others had. There were some who could not see the land till an hour afterwards. The inexperienced must first *learn*, before they will know *how* to see land. The first light-house (one sixty miles from Queenstown) came into view at 9:35 a. m. We passed it at 10:00 o'clock.

White sea-gulls come one or two days' journey into the sea to meet the ships, and follow them for food. These had been increasing from an early hour, and amounted to about fifty in number in the afternoon. It seems as if their wings would never tire. All day long they fly after the ships, sometimes even coming over the deck near the passengers.

A great excitement prevailed on board during the whole day, because a number of our passengers were to leave us there. While these were getting ready to depart, and bidding good-by to their many friends on board, many of us were busy writing letters to our friends and relatives in America. Those letters were taken on to Queenstown, there mailed, and brought the first news of our safe passage across the Atlantic. We were still a day from Liverpool, but it was a day of pleasure. The dangers of the deep were now forgotten, the strong winds of the Ocean had abated, and health and happiness over all on board prevailed. Our course continued along

THE COASTS OF IRELAND AND WALES.

At about 4:00 o'clock p. m., the little steamer "Lord Lyons" came up to our ship to fetch the passengers that were bound for Queenstown. A company of fruit-women came on board with gooseberries, raspberries and many other good things with which they fed our famished passengers. These were our first fruits of the season, and were highly relished by all.

The vegetation of Ireland is remarkable for its fresh, green color. We all agreed that we had never seen such a rich green color before. "Emerald Isle" (the *green island*) is a very appropriate name for Ireland. We saw many light-houses and beautiful castles hanging upon the rocky shores or standing proudly upon commanding eminences. Steamers keep so close to the shore in sailing from Queenstown to Liverpool, that the land is nearly always in sight. On Sunday morning, July 4th, the charming fields of Ireland had been exchanged for the lofty mountains of Wales. We passed Holyhead at 9:00 o'clock, and Liverpool came into sight at 1:30 p. m. An hour later we came so near to the coast that the individual trees of a shady wood upon the shores could readily be discerned. By 3:25 we had entered the Mersey, and "half-speed" was ordered. Five minutes later, we anchored and were touched by a tender. Here we learned what custom-house officers are for. Every trunk, carpet-bag and satchel had to be opened for them, and their busy hands were run all through our wardrobes. In order to detect any smuggling that might be attempted, they will examine every trunk or chest, &c., from top to bottom. They did not search our pockets, however, but short of that they are required to do most anything disagreeable to the traveler. As it was Sunday, all the shipping was tessellated with the colors of every nation. It is a grand sight to see acres upon acres of ships so profusely decorated with flags that it seems as if the sky was ablaze with their brilliant colors. Our own "Manhattan" sailed proudly into port with twenty-six flags streaming from her mast-head and rigging.

After we had passed muster, we passed over a kind of bridge or gangway from the "Manhattan" into a little steamer that had come down the river to fetch us. How glad we were to leave the good old ship, and bound into the arms of another that promised to take us ashore in a very few minutes! It was a glorious time! We had come to regard the "Manhattan" as a prison-house, from which we had long desired to take our leave, if we only could. But now that the parting hour had come, how changed our feelings! As the little boat sailed away, we felt sorry to leave her, and commenced to call her by pet names. "Good-by dear "Manhattan," many thanks to you for carrying us so safely across the deep wide sea," cried many of us; while others gave the customary *three cheers* and waved their hats. Though we left her empty behind—no friends, and no acquaintances remaining there, still we continued to wave our handkerchiefs at her so long as we could see her, and have ever since remembered her as the noblest of all the ships that was in harbor that day. Her colors seemed the brightest, and a hundred happy passengers separated that hour that will never cease to sing her praises. Permit me, kind reader, to add one line more, and in that line make mention of

LIFE-BOAT, NO. 5.

You may not be able to understand it, or to appreciate how a small party of our passengers came to regard her as almost a sacred thing, but there are a few that know the spell, and who will ever bless the page that tells the tale! Thither we went when the winds blew harder and the waves rolled higher, when our heads became heavier and our steps unsteady! She hung at or near the center of the ship, where there was the least rocking or swinging of all places in the whole vessel. During day-time we lay down beneath her shade, and at night, we would sit by her side relating to each other our feelings and experiences, &c. When sea-sickness had left our company, we agreed upon that place as our general rendezvous by day and by night, for the remainder of the voyage. There we spent our days and there we met every night! If our sleep was interrupted by a storm at the midnight hour, thither would we go for relief! A thousand recollections gather around that boat, and bind our hearts together there, as with so many cords; because our hearts meet there in fond remembrance, therefore will we never forget the place.

STEPPING ASHORE.

I had bid adieu to all my acquaintances before leaving the steamer, and consequently went ashore quite by myself. I did not experience that piercing thrill through my system as I had expected to, on touching the firm earth again; for we had seen the shore so long before we could land, that all its novelty had disappeared.

CHAPTER II.

LIVERPOOL.

Traveling-bag in hand, which contained my entire wardrobe, I now went in search of an hotel. The "Angel Hotel" was soon pointed out to me, and on entering it, I learned that several of my fellow-passengers had already taken rooms there. It is entirely under the control of ladies, being managed by a proprietress and female clerks. The house is an excellent one, and the accommodations are first-class. It bears a very appropriate name. After partaking of a hardy supper, I walked out to "take a look at Europe!" At 6:45 p. m., I entered St. Peter's Church, and was conducted to a pew. Here, as elsewhere in Europe, the young and the old of both sexes occupy the same seat together. One of the little boys of the family occupying the same pew with me, gave me a hymnbook. A part of the exercises consisted in chanting psalms. The eagle lectant and the Bible characters represented in the stained glass of the windows, soon enlisted my attention, but the meaning of having two birds perched upon a high stand in the middle of the church, I could not unfold, nor was there any one about that could tell me. The next day I saw the same bird beside a noble female form in the museum. "What bird is that?" said

I to a by-stander. "That figure," said he, "is the emblem of Liverpool, and the bird is the *liver*, which abounded down in the pools, and after which the place was first named."

St. Luke's was visited after service. The chorister seemed much pleased to meet an American, and showed me every mark of attention. When asked whether all the churches of Liverpool had their chancels in the *east* ends, he answered in the affirmative. I afterwards found this to be true all over Europe. The dead are buried everywhere so as to face the rising sun.

Around St. John's the memorial slabs lie flat upon the graves. IHS, with a cross over the H, is engraved upon the tombstones of the Catholics. These same letters IHS equivalent to JES or JESUS, are to be seen in almost every church and chapel in all Christian Europe. Upon goblets, chrismatories and crosses in the churches they are generally written in gold; while myriads of crosses on headstones in the graveyards bear the same mystical letters. Various other interpretations are given to them by different writers, but every explanation except the one above given, seems far-fetched and of doubtful origin, to say the least.

In summer, the sun sets after 8:00 o'clock in the latitude of Liverpool. I saw some twilight after 10:00 o'clock. The early dawn becomes visible before 2:00 o'clock in the morning, and he who wants to see the sun rise, must content himself with a short night. The Exchange is one of the most elegant buildings of its class in Europe. St. George's Hall contains the largest organ in England. In front of it are the Colossal Lions and the *Equestion Statue* of *Prince Albert. Britania* (England's crest) which surmounts the dome of the Town Hall, and the Wellington Statue, both face *south.*

I had expected to see people dressed differently in Liverpool from what is customary in America. In this and a dozen other anticipations I was utterly disappointed. Thus I was surprised at every step, because I was not surprised.

It was a scource of great grief to me that I could not indulge in refreshments on Sunday evening. A passenger after landing, is much like a patient after the fever has left him, he is hungry all the time. I had some American silver in my pocket, which I repeatedly offered to exchange for cakes, fruits and refreshments, at the numerous stores and stands which I passed, but no one was willing to invest in my stock of change. Thus I had to suffer both from hunger and thirst, because I did not have the right kind of money. On Monday I drew my check in English currency, and bought a suitable purse; but I was very awkward for a few days at counting money. England has the oddest and most irregular money table that I found from there to Egypt, except those of Holland and Germany. Many of the coins are old and purse-worn, so that it is impossible to decipher either the image or the superscription (Matt. XXII. 20), consequently the value must be guessed by their size.

I spent a great part of the day in the Museum. It contains a large and well classified collection of natural history, of objects of ancient and medieval art, of ancient manuscripts, of coins, of pictures, sculpture, &c. Saw the horns of a South African ox, each of which was about four feet long and five or six inches thick.

THE WONDERFUL CLOCK OF JACOB LOVELACE.

In the second story of the building stands a magnificent clock, weighing half a ton. Its case is about five feet long by three feet wide, and ten feet high. Upon its face are seven hands. It is a very old and complicated machine, and near it in a frame I found the following description: "It is the work of Jacob Lovelace, of Exeter, ornamented with Oriental figures and finely executed paintings, guilted by fretworks. The movements are 1st—A moving Panorama descriptive of Day and Night, Day is beautifully represented by Apollo in his Car, drawn by four spirited coursers, accompanied by the twelve hours, and Diana in her Car, drawn by stags attended by twelve hours, represents Night. 2nd—Two Guilt Figures in Roman costume who turn their heads and salute with their swords as the Panorama revolves; and also move in the same manner while the bells are ringing. 3rd—A Perpectual Almanac showing the day.

of the month on a semi-circular plate, the Index returning to the first day of the month on the close of each month, without alteration even in leap years, regulated only once in 130 years. 4th—A Circle, the Index of which shows the day of the week with its appropriate planet. 5th—A Perpetual Almanac showing the days of the Month Weekly and the Equation of time. 6th—A Circle showing the leap year, the Index revolving once in four years. 7th—A Time Piece that strikes the hours and chimes the quarters, on the face of which the whole of the twenty-four hours (twelve day and twelve night) are shown and regulated; within this circle the sun is seen in his course, with the time of rising and setting by an Horison receding or advancing as the days lengthen and shorten, and under is seen the moon showing her different quarters, phases, age, &c. 8th—Two female figures, one on each side of the Dial Plate, representing Fame and Terpsichore, who move in time when the organ plays. 9th—A Movement regulating the Clock as a repeater to strike or be silent. 10th—Saturn, the God of Time, who beats in movement while the organ plays. 11th—A circle of the face shows the names of eight celebrated tunes played by the organ in the interior of the cabinet every four hours. 12th—A Belfry with six ringers, who ring a merry peal *ad libitum;* the interior of this part of the cabinet is ornamented with beautiful paintings, representing some of the principal ancient Buildings of the city of Exeter. 13th—Connected with the organ there is a Bird Organ, which plays when required. This unrivaled piece of mechanism was perfectly cleaned and repaired by *W. Frost*, of Exeter, a self-taught artist. Jacob Lovelace, the maker, ended his days in great poverty in Exeter, at the age of sixty years, having been thirty-four years in completing it. This museum also contains glass of the Roman period—A. D. 100–500. The best specimens are a little greenish, but quite clear. One of the Egyptian mummies is wrapped up by a bandage of cloth, that was woven 3,000 years ago. It is still in a good state of preservation.

Tuesday, July 6th. The Sultan of Zanzibar, who was on a tour of inspection, started from the Northwestern Hotel at about 10:00 o'clock to drive out to the docks. He was accompanied by two natives from his own country, and the mayor and thirteen British cavaliers. The appearance, in Liverpool, of this South African dignitary, created a considerable sensation.

CHAPTER III.

CHESTER.

At 10:45 I left Liverpool for Chester. Edge Hill Tunnel, which is about a mile or a mile and a quarter in length, was passed in five minutes. Grain ripens from one to two months later here, than in Pennsylvania. The farmers were busy making hay, and the wheat still retained a dark green color. Harvesting is done in August and September. Wheat, rye, barley and potatoes are the staple products. No corn is cultivated in northern England. Wood is so scarce and dear in Great Britain, as well as upon the continent, that the farmers can not afford to build rail-fences. Hedge-fences, walls and ditches, therefore, take their places in every European country. All this is new to the American when he first comes to the Old World. Pass some fields of clover still in bloom. See men mow with the same "German" scythes that we use in America. We reached Chester before noon. This is one of the oldest cities, if not the oldest in the country. Here one sees the England of his dreams, the England he so long desired to see, and which now presents to his gaze, as it were in a focus, both the monuments and the rubbish of many ages. It was once a great military station of the Romans in Britain, who called it the City of

Legions. King Æthelfrith reduced it to ruins in the year 607, and it remained "a waste chester" (a waste castra or fortification) for three centuries. The Danes made its walls a stronghold against Alfred and Æthelred, and the Lady of the Mercians, who was the daughter of Alfred and the wife of Æthelred, recognized the importance of the place, and built it up again. It was the last city in England to hold out against William the Conqueror. During the Civil Wars the city adhered to the royal cause, and was besieged and taken by the Parliamentary forces in 1645. The *Phœnix Tower* bears the incription: *King Charles stood on this tower September* 24, 1645, *and saw his army defeated on Rowton Moor.*

The Rows are a very curious feature of the two principal streets running at right angles to each other. Besides the ordinary walks or pavements of these streets, there is a continuous covered gallery through the front of the second story. Some one has said, "Great is the puzzle of the stranger as to whether the roadway is down in the cellar, or he is upstairs on the landing, or the house has turned outside of the window." On this "upstairs street," as some call it, are situated all the first-class shops, the others being in the lower story on a level with the road. Picture to yourself a row of houses having porches in the second story but not in the first, and you have a correct idea of the Rows of Chester. To compare them to the

Arcades of Rue de Rivoli in Paris, is a mistake, as they do not resemble those more, than a porch over a pavement resembles one in the second story.

The Cathedral is a grand old church. It was built in the latter part of the twelfth and the beginning of the thirteenth centuries, upon the same site where two of its predecessors had already crumbled into decay. "*St. John's Church* is even more ancient than the Cathedral, having been built in the eleventh century. I shall never forget its weather-beaten walls and its mossy roof. In many places, the thickness of the walls is greatly reduced by the rain and hail that have washed and beaten against it *so* long. In my rambles through Chester I had the good fortune of meeting and forming the acquaintance of an Irish Catholic Priest and a wine merchant from Wolverhampton, two intelligent and amiable gentlemen, who taught me much about those curious relics still found in heaps among the ruins of old Chester. At about 2:00 o'clock we stood upon the high square tower of St. John's (thirty-five feet each side at the top) amidst the elderberries and grass which flourish at that giddy height. Looking at the town from this elevation, one gets no idea of its *unique* features, as the numerous slate-roofs give it the appearance of a modern town. The descent was made with difficulty, and even attended with some danger, for the long wooden stairs or ladders are becoming shaky and a break of one of its steps might precepitate one from such a height that instant death was the most desirable alternative. But who would not become bold, or even sometimes more that, amid such surroundings! When one says we *can't* get there, another is sure to declare that we *must* get there! "What! would you come so far to see antiquity, and then count your steps how near you would approach her?" Eight bells constitute the peal in this venerable old tower. Near by, stand the ivy-clad and moss-covered ruins of portions of the sacred edifices that date back, even to the earlier ages of the Christian era, and from among the dust and rubbish are picked up the broken images of hideous-looking idols that were the ornaments (?) of the temples once standing there. We found a large collection of those ghastly-looking idols piled away in the crypt of the church. Whether the emblems of Druid, or Christian worship, these "images cut out of stone" evidently represent an age, in which the heart was subdued by superstitious fear rather than by "*love.*"

The Walls merit especial attention. They still surround the city completely, and form, in a certain sense, the proudest and most admirable promenade that the world affords anywhere. From it are obtained the best views of the Cathedral and of the country around. The ascent to it is made by a flight of steps on the north side of the Eastgate. A ditch or canal about twenty-five feet wide, runs all around the wall and used to render the battering of the wall a matter of extreme difficulty before the invention of powder and the introduction of fire-arms. The pavement, on top of the wall, is four and a half to six feet wide, and skirted on both sides by thinner walls; that on the outside being about four or five feet high. From behind this wall the soldiers would hurl spears, javelins, &c., at the attacking enemy, and keep them in check. How things have changed since that time! Now this walk forms the peaceful and delightful promenade of the private citizens. Here meet the young and the gay, fashion displays its gaudiest colors, and lovers take their "moonlight strolls."

Such is the use now made of the Walls of Chester! America has no walled cities; Europe has but few without walls. In the early history of Europe, every town even had its walls. In many places where the walls have almost disappeared, there are still remaining the gates of the city. At those points the walls were made doubly strong, and high and impregnable towers built over them, in which were stationed strong guards "to defend the gates." Then no stranger could enter without some kind of "pass" from recognized authorities. Did not the system of "pass-ports" which has been handed down to our day, but which seems to be falling into disuse even in Europe, have its origin in this way? At 5:40 I left Chester for Birmingham. On our way we passed Crewe, one of the great railroad centers of England. At this station *five hundred* trains pass each other every twenty-four hours.

We arrived at Birmingham at 8:45 p. m. Between Wolverhampton and Birmingham lies the great ore and manufacturing district of England. Ore-beds and smoke-stacks cover all the area some thirty miles long and sixteen miles wide, except that occupied by the miserable cottages (some of them mere hovels) of the laborers. Looking at this immense area from the cars, it presents the appearance of one continuous town. No wonder that England can accommodate a population of some twenty odd millions on an area but little more than that of Pennsylvania, when poor humanity is thus crowded together. In the cars, I had formed the acquaintance of a sociable party of ladies and gentlemen, who pointed out places to me, and instructed me concerning the manners and social habits of the people. From Liverpool hither, I found very small brick houses the rule, and spacious buildings like our Pennsylvania farm houses, the exception. Barns, I saw none; small stables supply their places even on large farms. We saw several very fine castles by the way, however.

Birmingham is known as "the toy-shop of Europe," "but most of the toys are for children of larger growth." One can nowhere see richer sights than in the show-rooms of many of these shops. One that I visited, a glass show-room containing chandeliers priced upwards of a thousand dollars, and all varieties of fancy-wares of every description, had large mirrors at the ends of the room, covering the entire walls, and producing the grandest effect conceivable. The objects in the room were thus infinitely multiplied in both directions, so that whichever way one turned his face, glittering glass-ware was seen "as far as the eye could reach."

Such sights are simply bewildering! It is a little difficult to gain admittance to the manufacturing departments of many of these places, but to literary characters that represent "newspapers," the doors are generally opened quite readily. In hunting these shops, I discovered a great want of system in the naming and numbering of the streets of this otherwise quite elegant city. I had passed a certain street twice, from end to end, in search of a particular number. Upon further inquiry, I learned that what I had considered one street, was numbered and named as two, though there was not the slightest deviation from a perfectly straight line at any point of it. To make bad worse, the houses were counted and numbered upwards on one side of the street, and downwards on the other side. In such a city the stranger must find places by *speculation!*

Strange things one meets at every step in Europe,

and soon gets so used to it, that it seems the strangest to see something that is not strange; but oddities are perhaps no plentier on one side of the Atlantic than they are on the other, and are equally amusing everywhere. Upon the burial ground of St. Philip's, stands a monument in honor and memory of a wife that died at the age of fifty-nine years, which has a bee-hive and the inscription: "She looked well to the ways of her household, and did not eat the bread of idleness."

A number of fine statues adorn some of the public squares. One of these, a bronze statue to *Peel* faces *east;* while *Priestley's* marble statue faces *south.*

The first thing that arrests the tourist's attention on arriving at Birmingham, is its magnificent railroad station, the largest and finest that I had thus far met with in England. As it was late in the evening when I arrived, I had no time to pay much attention to it until the next day. The part entered by the trains is about 1,050 feet long and 200 feet wide, all in one apartment. This part is sprung by forty-two immense iron arches, supporting a roof half of whose covering is glass. The numerous tracks are separated by platforms running lengthwise through the building, from which the passengers enter the cars. In order to avoid the danger of crossing the tracks, there is a fine foot-bridge, eighteen feet wide, running across the tracks above the reach of the locomotive stacks.

From this bridge, stairs descent to the platforms between the tracks, as before mentioned. Three hundred trains pass through this station every twenty-four hours. An officer receives and dismisses these trains by means of a signal-bell. The ticket-offices are in the second story of a large building adjoining.

RAILROADS IN EUROPE.

There are no "conductors" upon the trains after they leave the "stations" (which, by the way, I never heard any one call depots, in Europe) but officers are stationed at the head of every stairway to punch the tickets. Five minutes before any particular train leaves, the ticket-office is closed, and the conductors pass through the cars and inspect the tickets. If any one did come into a wrong car or train, there is still time left to correct the mistake. Tickets are not collected till one's destination is reached, where they *must* be delivered to the door-keeper on leaving the station. Without it, a passenger is a prisoner. "Railroading" is so perfectly systemized in Europe, that it is quite impossible either to cheat a company, or to be cheated out of one's time by missing trains. There is little danger of missing a train even in countries where one can not speak the language. The cars are divided into compartments (*Ger. Abtheilungen*) of two seats or benches each, running across the car, with doors at the sides. In 1st Class cars, the seats are finely cushioned and the compartments are about as inviting in appearance as our Palace cars; in 2nd Class cars the seats are comfortable but common; but 3rd Class cars have only bare wooden benches. There are in some countries, 4th Class cars, which have no seats. I did not see any of those, but from what I learned of others, they must resemble our freight cars. In those, too, passengers have the privilege of standing or sitting down, according to their taste or comfort. Tickets to 1st Class cars cost about the same as in this country, 2nd Class tickets cost three-fourths, and 3rd Class about half as much.

In hilly sections of the country, the railways generally cross the wagon roads by bridges; but wherever the two kinds of roads intersect each other on a level, travel on the latter is interrupted by gates and watchmen, who permit no one to pass while a train is approaching the crossing. Thus every railway crossing in Europe is superintended day and night by watchmen. These watchmen are noticed by signal-bells, at the departure of every train running in the direction of their crossings. Under such a system, accidents are impossible. Even the doors of each "compartment" are barred by the conductors before the trains are dismissed, and will not be opened by the conductors of the next station, until the train stands still. The tickets, besides containing the ordinary matter on tickets in this country, have also the price printed upon them.

Some of the stations of the Old World, are buildings of extraordinary beauty and magnificence.

The grandest structure of this kind, is, probably, the station (Ger. *Station* or *Bahnhof*, Italian *Stazione*) of Stuttgart. Among many others, might also be mentioned the stations of Paris, of Turin, of Milan and of Rome; but the Great Western Station of London, takes the palm of those all, for magnificence, beauty and convenience combined. What the station at Clapham (seven miles above London) looks like, I do not know, but it is said, that from 1,000 to 1,200 trains run through it every twenty-four hours! What multitudes of people must be streaming over the platforms and past the windows of the ticket-offices of such a station, every day! At Birmingham and at Crewe, where 300 and 500 trains pass daily, the swarming thousands remind one of *floods* and *inundations*, but how must it look at Clapham?

July 7th, 3:40 p. m. Leave Birmingham for Stratford on the Avon (pron. ā'von).

CHAPTER IV.

STRATFORD-UPON-AVON.

Arrived at 5:00 p. m., July 7th. It had been my intention to pay this place only a brief visit, giving but a glance at "The Poet's" home and birthplace, and then start on foot for Coventry; but I soon found that Stratford possesses more charms than I had anticipated. Shakespeare's fame has an influence over his native town, that is simply marvelous.

The thousands of tourists that come from every land, and from every clime, *to see the scenes that the poet saw, and breath the same air that he breathed,* make the place one of the most popular resorts of literary pilgrims, that can be found anywhere.

The buildings of Stratford are small and low, as is the rule, rather than the exception, in English towns and villages. Many are covered with tiles, but the thatch roof is also very common here. This consists of a mixture of straw and earth, often more than a foot in thickness, and covered with moss and grass. Notwithstanding this, both the houses and the streets are kept remarkably clean and inviting; so much so, that I felt nowhere else so soon and so perfectly at home as here. Its people seem to be possessed of every virtue, and preëminent among them all, is that of hospitality which seems to be blooming in the hearts of all its citizens to-day, as did poetry in the mind of Shakespeare three hundred years ago.

The streets of this town are kept as clean as a floor, by sweepers watching the streets all day long, collecting and carrying away all the refuse matter. One day, I felt ill at ease about a small piece of paper that had become a superfluity in my pocket, but which I was afraid to throw upon the street, as it would there seem as much out of place as if I should drop it upon the carpet in a parlor. I passed along the pavement with it, until I met a street-sweeper, and there threw it upon his heap with a nod, which he reciprocated with a bow.

On entering Stratford, my foot first tended toward

SHAKESPEARE'S BIRTHPLACE,

a large two-story house, about fifty feet long, having three large dormer-windows and two chimneys, one of them running up on the outside of the house.

The custodian takes the visitor through every apartment of it, giving the history of the same and of numerous articles of furniture and Shakesperian relics, &c., which constitute a considerable museum.

When William Shakespeare's father was a "well-to-do" man, he occupied the whole house; but after he had become poor, the east end was rented to a hotel-keeper, and he lived in the middle part only, which has later been used as a butcher-shop.

"On the 16th of September, 1847, it (the building) was put up for sale by the magniloquent Mr. George Robins, and in consequence of a strong appeal to the feelings of the people, made through the public press, by which a *National Subscription* was raised for the purpose; this house was bought at the bidding of Mr. Peter Cunningham, for something more than 3,000 pounds sterling, and was placed under Trustees on behalf of the Nation."

Space will not permit me to make mention of more than a few of the many interesting books, manuscripts, works of art, antiques and relics, found in this Library and Museum. Among them stands the desk at which little "Willie" sat at school, also a ring which he wore at his thumb (later in life), and upon which are engraved the letters "W. S." and a "true lover's knot." I spent nearly an hour here, a studying how things looked in Shakespeare's time. The ground floors of the house, are covered with flag-stones broken in varied forms, as accident would have it, while the rough massive timbers of the floors above stand out unpainted and unplastered. After taking a pleasant walk, with a gay party, through the garden, in which are cultivated all the flowers of which Shakespeare speaks in his works, and, (I must not fail also to mention), after having taken our turns in sitting upon *Shakespeare's chair*, I bade the sociable company "good-by!" and started for

SHOTTERY,

"a genuine country village, consisting of a few

straggling farm-houses and brick and timber cottages, standing apart from each other in their old gardens and orchard-crofts. Simple, old-fashioned, and almost untouched by the innovations of modern life, we are here amidst the charmed past of Shakespeare's time." Here is still to be seen, the cottage in which was born and lived Anne Hathaway, the wife of Wm. Shakespeare. This village lies about a mile from Stratford, and is approached by a pleasant walk across quiet and fertile fields and pasture lands, the same path along which "Willie" used to steal when he went a-wooing his Anne. The Hathaway cottage is a large old-fashioned thatch-roofed building—very plain but very homely. The clumsy string-lifted wooden door-latches, and the wooden pins fixing the framing, and which have never been cut off, but stick up some inches from the wall, are still all there. It was dusk before I got there. My rap at the door was responded to by the appearance of an old lady custodian, a descendent of the Hathaway family, who immediately busied herself to light a tallow candle. That being successfully accomplished, she commenced her story by pointing out the old hearth, and explaining the kitchen arrangements of olden times. Among the old articles of furniture, is a plain wooden settee or bench which used to stand outside against the house near the door, during the summer, and which, as tradition has it, was Willie's and Anne's courting settee.

Pictures of their courtships hang against the walls, exhibiting styles and fashions well in keeping with the antique furniture of the room. An old carved bed-stead of the Shakespeare era, stands in the room above. Here the custodian offered me a book of autographs, asking me to sign my name, as has been customary since October 4th, 1846. Six books have been filled with autographs, since that time. Among the signatures I saw one Emma R., July 24th, 1866. "This," said the custodian, "is the signature of the Queen of the Sandwich Islands."

Henry W. Longfellow's signature, who was here with his brother (and families), June 23rd, 1868, and that of Chas. Dickens, here in 1852, were also pointed out.

The old lady would not let me go away without having taken a drink from "the spring where Anne used to drink." After presenting me with "lavender" and "rosemary" for mementoes, and a button-hole boquet consisting of a fine rose and buds, for immediate display, she wished me god-speed on my journey, and I retraced the path across the fields to Stratford.

New Place, the Home of Shakespeare, is the most charming place in all Stratford. The extensive yard and garden which belonged to the property in Shakespeare's time, had been partially cut up in lots and covered with houses; but these have all been removed again, and the grounds laid out into walks, lawns and flower beds, as the poet was wont to have them. His yard and garden covered an area of about two acres. The gentleman who has charge of the property now, exerts himself to the utmost, to make the surroundings pleasant and inviting, aiming particularly to plant the same trees and flowers that the poet had planted there, and to keep his favorite trees, or lineal successors of them, in the same sites. Among the ornamental trees and flowers, he pointed out a number that he obtained from Vick, the florist, of Rochester, N. Y.

Shakespeare was buried in the Church of the Holy Trinity. His wife, his only daughter Susanna and her husband, Thomas Nash, lie with him in the same row, immediately in front of the altar-rails. His tombstone bears the following inscription:

GOOD FREND FOR JESVS SAKE FORBEARE,
TO DIGG THE DVST ENCLOASED HEARE:
BLESE BE $\overset{E}{Y}$ MAN $\overset{T}{Y}$ SPARES THES STONES,
AND CVRST BE HE $\overset{T}{Y}$ MOVES MY BONES.

The only typographical peculiarity not rendered here, is the grouping together of HE in HEARE and TH in THES, after the fashion of monograms.

This church also contains a half-length figure of Shakespeare, painted after nature. There is evidence extant that it had already taken its place against the wall in the year 1623. Beneath is inscribed:

> Judicio pylivm genio socratem, arte maronem,
> Terra tegit, popvlvs mæret, Olympvs Habet.*

Stay, passenger; why goest thov by so fast?
Read, if thov canst, whom enviovs death hath plast
Within this monvment; Shakespeare, with whom
Quick natvre dide; whose name doth deck ys. tombe
Far more than cost; sith all yt. he hath writt
Leaves living art bvt page to serve his witt.

Obiit. Ano. Doi. 1616.
Ætatis 53. Die 23. Ap.

*[In judgment a Nestor, in genius a Socrates, in art a Virgil. The earth covers him, the people mourn for him, Olympus has him.]

Of the Guildhall, the Grammar School, and the beautiful Avon, with their hundred sweet associations, I dare say nothing more. After a stay of three days, during which time I had recovered from the effects of the severe strain and close application of mind and body, by which both had suffered exhaustion, and been driven almost to the verge of prostration, in the museum at Liverpool and the ruins of Chester; I started on way to Warwick (pron. War'rick) and Coventry. As my purpose was to walk the whole distance, about twenty miles, I sent my sachel by rail, to the former place.

CHAPTER V.

STRATFORD TO COVENTRY.

This is the walk referred to by the two Englishmen who laid a wager as to which was the finest walk in England. "After the money had been put up, one named the walk from Stratford to Coventry, and the other from Coventry to Stratford. How the umpire decided the case, is not recorded." It was late in the afternoon on Saturday, July 10th, when I bade adieu to Stratford, and went away rejoicing, in the hope of soon seeing the beauties of England's most charming agricultural section.

After two hours, I entered Charlecote Park, where I disturbed several herds of deer, some hundred head in all. From this park, as lame tradition has it, Shakespeare once stole deer, and became an exile for the crime!

On Sunday forenoon I attended service at

ST. MARY'S CHURCH,

in Warwick. The choir, lady chapel and chapter-house are among the purest examples of Decorated work, and date from 1394. The tomb of Richard Beauchamp (Bee'cham) in the Lady Chapel, is considered the most splendid in the kingdom, with the single exception of that of Henry VII. in Westminster Abbey.

A very high tower stands over the entrance door, at the west end of the church. The organ and choir (at the same end) rendered the finest music that I heard in England. There were several very highly cultivated voices among those of the half dozen ladies that occupied the space in front of the organ.

Everything else about the services is eminently examplary of the olden times. Preaching is the least important part of the exercises. Pulpit oratory finds no place here. Singing, praying and readings are the leading feature of worship in the English Church in general, and of old churches like this, in particular. Such exercises seem to be eminently appropriate for a people whose hearts and minds are almost petrified in civil and religious forms and ceremonies. The step which the English Church took away from Catholicism, must have been an extremely short one, if it was a step at all. This congregation still turn their faces toward the east, during a certain part of their recitals, and bow ceremoniously, in concert, as often as they mention the name of "Jesus Christ."

Two miles from Warwich, is Leamington, (Lĕm'ington), a fashionable "spa," which I visited in the afternoon. It is a very pretty town, and emphatically modern in style; presenting nothing that is anti-American in appearance, except its clusters of chimney-tops, so common everywhere in Europe. As soon as one has crossed the Atlantic he will seldom longer see single square tops built upon the chimneys, but each apartment of the house has its own chimney; all these converge, but do not meet before coming out of the roof, so that from two to six or eight tops generally keep each other company on the house-tops.

At 3:45 p. m., I started from Warwick for Coventry. The road leading from this place to Coventry is an excellent turnpike, just as that is from Stratford hither, and has a splendid gravel walk for pedestrians on one side, and a riding path for those on horse-back, on the other side.

Five miles brought me to Kenilworth Castle. Great must have been its glories when Elizabeth came here in 1575 to visit Liecester. Cromwell dismantled it, and laid waste the gardens around it, and the tooth of time has been gnawing at it ever since, but it is magnificent even in its ruins. "Go round about it, tell the towers thereof, and mark well its bulwarks, if you would know what a mighty fortress it must have been when it held out for half a year against Henry III. in 1266, or what a lordly palace when it thrice welcomed Elizabeth to its hospitalities, three hundred years later."

A quarter or half a mile further on, is a fine church, and near by an ivy-covered arch. A passing gentleman told me this had been the entrance to an ancient abbey; and others said it was a part of the ruined Castle of Kenilworth.

It was 6:00 o'clock when I left here, and had

five miles more to Coventry. A mile and a half on this side of that city lie the extensive possessions of Lord Leigh. This wealthy peer owns here, in one stretch, about twenty square miles of the finest and most fertile land in the world.

About a mile from Coventry I encountered an enormous stream of pedestrians coming out of the city to take their evening walk. The promenade, which is about ten feet wide at that place, was so thronged with the gay young couples, that I found it impossible to walk against the mighty stream, and took the middle of the street. After I had entered the gate, I found the pavements on both sides of the road becoming more and more crowded, all bound for a pleasant grassy grove known as "the lovers quarters."

It is difficult to make estimates under such circumstances, but there can hardly have been less than 5,000 to 10,000 persons upon the promenade that evening.

COVENTRY.

Coventry is remarkable for its elegant parish churches, which are among the finest in England.

"St. Michael's Church is one of the largest (some say *the* largest) and noblest parish churches in England." Its steeple built between 1373 and 1395, is 303 feet high. The church was finished in 1450, when Henry VI. heard mass there. The second and third of the "three tall spires" of Coventry are that of Trinity Church and of Christ

Church. St. John's is famous for its magnificen western window.

Coventry is well worth a visit on account ‹ those famous churches.

I was accompanied to those fine edifices by tw precociously intelligent little beauties, (of seven an eleven years respectively), whose gayety and chee: fulness not onlv rendered their society very accep able to "a stranger in a strange land;" but th simple fact of their being permitted to accompan so perfect a stranger to all parts of the city, showe how much trust some foreigners have in Amer cans, and consequently, to what extent one ma put confidence in them. Such incidents are ver pleasant and encouraging to the lonely pilgrin and may be made a matter of almost daily occu rence by any social but circumspective travele The traveling public in Europe are so social, an etiquette so free, that the tourist can at every ste form the acquaintance of some one who is boun for the same church, museum or pleasure garde: and thus be continually enjoying the benefits intelligent and cheerful company.

On Monday noon, July 12th, I left Coventry b rail, to return to

WARWICK VIA LEAMINGTON.

At 3:30 p. m., I had passed through the man elegant apartments of Warwick Castle, and stoc at the top of its tower, overlooking the wood groves, and flower garden, occupying the 7(

cres of ground belonging to that princely mansion. Among the ornamental trees, our guide pointed ut "one that Queen Victoria planted with her wn hands." Scott calls Warwich Castle "the airest monument of ancient and chivalrous splen- or which yet remains uninjured by time."

It is said to have been founded in the 10th cen- ury, destroyed in the 13th, and restored by Thomas e Beauchamp in the 14th. It has been preserved o well that it looks almost like a new palace, to-day

OXFORD

vith its score of colleges scattered all over the city, onstituting the world renowned University of the ame name, was "done" the next day, but done in hurry. It is a depressing business to pass by so nuch, giving but a glance here and there, and not e able to see so many things more at leisure. Magnificent libraries and museums, grand churches nd chapels, and extensive buildings and botanical ardens, were rushed through and passed by, as if he charm and beauty of Oxford's scenes consisted ather in making the images of them flit in quick uccession across the retina of the eye, than in ex- mining, studying and contemplating them.

Merton College, founded 1264, contains a library 00 years old. Many of its large and rare books re chained to their respective shelves, like dogs o their kennels; and with chains too, of sufficient trength to check any canine's wanderings. Christ Church I entered by the Tower-Gate, so named after the great bell contained in the cupola of t tower over it. This bell weighs about 17,0 pounds. The quadrangle inclosed by the buil ings of this college, is "the largest and the mc noble in Oxford. Its dimensions are 264 by 2 feet, or nearly an acre and a half in extent. T "Hall" is 113 feet by forty, and fifty feet in heigl "The roof is of carved oak, with very elega pendants, profusely decorated with the armor bearings and badges of King Henry VIII. a Cardinal Wolsey, and has the date 1529." Its ba window at the end of the dais with its rich grain vault of fan-tracery, is admired by every one.

Christ Church Meadow, with its "Broad Wal one and a quarter mile in circuit, and Addiso walk, near St. Mary Magdalen College, are amo the most bewitching promenades that can be fou anywhere, while "the manner in which Hig street opens upon the view, in walking from t Botanic Garden, is probably one of the finest thir of the kind in Europe."

Oxford is all history and poetry. There is tradition that upon the top of the elegant tower St. Mary Magdalen, formerly on every May-d morning, at four o'clock, was sung a requiem the soul of Henry VII., the reigning monarch the time of its erection. The custom of chanti a hymn beginning with

"Te Deum Patrem colimus,
Te laudibus prosequimur,"

the same place is still preserved, on the same ɔrning of each year, at five o'clock.

The dark lantern which Guy Fawks used in the ɪnpowder Plot in 1605, and a picture of the con-irators are contained in the New Museum.

From Oxford I went directly to London by a ɜt line, which occupied less than two hours in aking the journey. From the cars, we saw indsor Castle, with its colors raised, meaning that e Queen was there.

We also passed some large patches of flowers in e fields, which were cultivated for the London ›wer-market.

Foreigners in general have a great passion for ›wers. While ladies wear them in their hair, ›on their bosoms, and carry them in their hand, e gentlemen will carry button-hole bouquets, and ɪny even stick them upon their hats. They are ɜhionable with all ages and all classes. From ɔoming maidenhood to gray-headed age, all will orn themselves with flowers. The English seem *cultivate* the most flowers, while the French and e Italians, and (lately ?) the Germans, *wear most* ›on their persons. In England, every available ɔt of spare soil about the yard, is planted with ›wers; on the continent, all the fashionable res-urants and cafes must daily be supplied with ɜsh bouquets, with which these halls are decorated lavish profusion.

CHAPTER VI.

LONDON.

We now approach London, the mighty mistres of the commercial world, the most populous cit on our globe. Here, certers the trade of all nation: here, is transacted the business of the world.] you would know how it looks where concentratio of business has reached its climax, then come t London. Many of its streets are so crowdod wit omnibuses, wagons, dray-carts, &c., that it is almo impossible for a pedestrian to cross them. Whe the principal streets intersect each other, the bust and tumult of trade is so great, that it becomes dangerous undertaking to attempt to effect a cros ing at such a square.

For the protection and accommodation of tho on foot, the squares are provided with little pla forms elevated a step above the surface of the roa and surrounded with a thick row of stone post between these, the pedestrian can enter, but the shield him from the danger of being tread und the feet of horses, or run over by vehicles. He one stands perfectly safe, even when everything confusion for an acre around. As soon as an o portunity opens, he runs to the next landing; ar thus continues, from landing to landing, until tl opposite side of the square is reached. It oft equires five minutes to accomplish this feat. It ıas been estimated that no less than 20,000 teams .nd equestrians, and 107,000 pedestrians cross Lon- lon Bridge every twenty-four hours. By police .rrangement, slow traffic travel at the sides and the [uick in the center. It is 928 feet long and fifty- 'our wide. Not only are the streets crowded, but)eneath the houses and streets, in the dark bosom ›f the earth, there is a net-work of

UNDERGROUND RAILROADS,

:xtending to all parts of the city, which pick up hat surplus of travel which it has become impos- .ible to accomplish above.

There are some thirty miles of tunneled rail- vays in London, now, and the work of extending hem is carried on with increasing energy. This 'ailway is double track everywhere, and forms two :ircuits, upon one of which the trains continually 'un in one direction, while those on the other track :un in the opposite direction. Collisions are there- 'ore impossible between these two systems of :ounter-currents. Numerous stations are built all ılong these roads, where travelers can descend to neet the trains or leave them, to make their ascend ;o the city above. To give the reader an idea of ;he immense amount of traveling done in these dark passages under London, it need only be stated that long trains of cars pass each station every "ten minutes," and are as well filled with passen- gers as those of railroads on the surface of the earth. The cars are comfortably lighted, so that after one has taken his seat and the train begins to run along, it resembles night-traveling so perfectly, that the difference is scarcely perceptible.

Of all modes of travel, these underground railroads afford the quickest, cheapest, safest and most convenient manner of transit.

This great metropolis includes the cities of London and Westminster, the borough of Southwark, and thirty-six adjacent parishes, precincts, townships, &c. It covers an area of 122 square miles, and has a population of about 4,000,000, that of the *City of London proper* being no more than about 75,000. Murray's Modern London contains the following statistics:

"The Metropolis is supposed to consume in one year 1,600,000 quarters of wheat, 300,000 bullocks, 1,700,000 sheep, 28,000 calves, and 35,000 pigs." (If these animals were arranged in a double line, they would constitute a drove over a thousand miles long!)

"One market alone (Leadenhall) supplies about 4,025,000 head of game. This, together with 3,000-000 of salmon, irrespective of other fish and flesh, is washed down by 43,200,000 gallons of porter and ale, 2,000,000 gallons of spirits, and 65,000 pipes of wine. To fill its milk and cream jugs, 13,000 cows are kept. To light it at night, 360,000 gas-lights fringe the streets, consuming, every twenty-four hours, 13,000,000 cubic feet of gas; while the private consumption of gas in a year amounts to 10,000,000,000 cubic feet. Its arterial or water system supplies the enormous quantity of 44,383,328 gallons per day, while its venous or sewer system carries off 9,502,720 cubic feet of refuse. To warm its people and to supply its factories, a fleet, amounting to upwards of a thousand sail, is employed in bringing annually 3,000,000 tons of coal, exclusive of 2,000,000 tons brought by rail. The thirsty souls of London need have no fear of becoming thirstier so long as there are upwards of 6,700 public houses and 2,000 wine merchants to minister to their deathless thirst.

"The bread to this enormous quantity of sack is represented by 2,500 bakers, 1,700 butchers, not including pork butchers, 2,600 tea dealers and grocers, 1,260 coffee-room keepers, nearly 1,500 dairy-men, and 1,350 tobacconists. To look after the digestion of this enormous amount of food upwards of 2,400 duly licensed practitioners, surgeons and physicians are daily running to and fro through this mighty metropolis, whose patients, in due course of time and physic, are handed over to the tender mercies of 500 undertakers. Nearly 3,000 boot and shoe-makers give their aid to keep our feet dry and warm, while 2,950 tailors do as much for the rest of our bodies. The wants of the fairer portion of the population are supplied by 1,080 linen drapers, 1,500 milliners and dressmakers; 1,540 private schools take charge of their children; and

290 pawn-brokers' shops find employment and profit out of the reverses, follies, and vices of the community. It is said that 700,000 *cats* are kept in London, to maintain whom large part of the 3,000 horses which die every week is sold by cat's-meat vendors. About 520,000 (1873) houses give shelter to upwards of three millions of people, whose little differences are aggravated or settled by upwards of 3,000 attorneys and 3,900 barristers.

"The spiritual wants of this mighty aggregate of human souls are cared for by more than 2,000 clergymen and dissenting ministers, who respectively preside over 620 churches and 423 chapels, of which latter buildings the Independents have 121, the Baptists 100, the Wesleyans 77, the Roman Catholics about 90, whereas in 1808 they had but 13, the Calvinists and English Presbyterians 10 each, the Quakers 7, and the Jews 10; the numerous other sects being content with numbers varying from one to five each. To wind up with the darkest part of the picture, the metropolis contains on an average 129,000 paupers."

On my way to London, I fell in company with a young gentleman who was well acquainted in the metropolis, and who gave me much valuable information, and assisted me in establishing myself in a central location, where excursions to all sections could be conveniently made. This was "King's Cross Station," the terminus of the Great Northern Railway, and one of the principal stations of the Metropolitan (or Underground) Railroad; besides, it is in the heart of the great city. We reached it by the Underground Railway from Paddington, the terminus of the Great Western Railway. When we *came up out of the earth* at Kings Cross, I saw a *busy-ness* such as I had never seen before. My friend went with me a short distance to point out a street where private rooms could be rented.

The tourist who wants to make the most of his time must never engage to board at his lodging-place, as it will be very inconvenient and at a sacrifice of much time, to return thither for his meals. The most economical way is to have a room either at a hotel or at a private house, and to take the meals at the numerous restaurants, one of which can be reached anywhere in five minutes.

I had great difficulty in procuring a room, but persisted in my inquiries until I succeeded. The traveler will learn quicker than any other person that *perseverence is the only road to success.* He must often see everything go contrary for a whole hour, and even sometimes for half a day in succession. Such reverses frequently occasion a "blue-Monday" in the middle of the week.

My first walk, after I had found a home in London, was to the Post-Office, to look for letters from my friends in America. This was about three miles off. I returned a different way, and took a look at the exterior of St. Paul's. As the Covent

Garden Theater (the finest in London) was already full before I reached it, I went on to the Oxford Street Music Theater and spent my first evening there. The next day (Wednesday, July 14th,) I entered

ST. PAUL'S CATHEDRAL,

the noblest building in England in the Classic style. Its length from east to west is 550 feet and its height to the top of the cross 370 feet. Under the dome is an area affording seats for 5,000 persons. Here 5,000 charity children are collected on the first Thursday in June every year, to unite their voices in songs of praise. Besides the dome, St. Paul's has two other towers, each 222 feet high. In one of these is the clock and the great bell upon which it strikes.

The length of the minute-hand of the clock is eight feet, and its weight seventy-five pounds; the length of the hour-hand is five feet five inches, and its weight forty-four pounds. The bell is ten feet in diameter and weighs 11,474 pounds. "It is inscribed, 'Richard Phelps made, me, 1716,' and is never used except for striking the hour, and for tolling at the deaths and funerals of any of the Royal Family, the Bishops of London, the Deans of St. Paul's, and the Lord Mayor, should he die in his mayoralty."

It requires a man three quarters of an hour every day to wind the clock, the striking weight alone weighing 1,200 pounds.

The dome constitutes a very remarkable whisper gallery, the slightest whisper being transmitted from one side to the other with the greatest distinctness.

This Cathedral contains many fine monuments interesting from the persons they commemorate. Among them are those to the Duke of Wellington, to Nelson, to Lord Cornwallis, to Sir Charles Napier, to Sir William Jones, the Oriental scholar, and numerous others.

CRYSTAL PALACE,

which is outside of the city, is perhaps the grandest Exposition Building in the world, and possibly the only structure of the kind in existence, since the destruction, by fire, of Crystal Palace, in New York. This Great Exhibition Building was first built upon Hyde Park, covering nearly nineteen acres of ground. It was visited by upwards of 6,000,000 persons during the twenty-four weeks that it was open, or about 40,000 persons daily. The receipts amounted to over $2,000,000.

It was re-erected and enlarged at Sydenham, in Kent, 1853–4, at a cost of over $7,000,000.

It must be over a quarter of a mile long, and about one-fourth as wide. The entire sides and the whole of the immense arched roof are of glass, admitting all the light except what little is intercepted by the sashes, thus affording an illumination quite equal to that outside, under the clear canopy of heaven.

The exterior gardens and water-works are magnificent. Among the attractions about the yard, is a glass tower about forty-five or fifty feet in diameter and over 200 feet high. Beautiful indeed is this magnificent crystal tower.

A clock with sixty-nine faces shows the times of so many different places on our planet. For the accommodation of such as are astronomically inclined, I render the following record as I entered it upon my diary, July 16th: Civil Middle Time, 12:40 p. m.; Astronomical Middle Time, 12:39½ p. m.; Sidereal Time, 19:49¾; True Time, 12:38½ p. m.

Around its great organ, there is seating accommodation for a choir of 2,000 singers.

For seeing the building only, one could well afford to go a great distance; but there are also constantly on exhibition a large collection of curiosities of every description, while extensive bazars expose for sale the richest and finest goods and wares of all kinds, and from the stores of every quarter of the globe.

There is also on exposition a large collection of plants, and a magnificent art gallery of paintings, sculpture, &c. Concert every day.

London has much fog and rain. I had but two fair days out of the eight I spent there. One very rainy morning I started out to see the Houses oi Parliament. On my way thither I came to Trafalgar Square. In the center stands the magnificent

Nelson Column, surrounded by statues and fountains. In order to shield myself from the rain, and to enjoy the view of the grand square before me, and of the Parliamentary Buildings in the distance, I took refuge upon the portico of the National Gallery of Paintings. Here I incidentally met and formed the acquaintance of the brother of Miss Rosie Hersee, a songstress, who had lately made herself popular in this country. After accompanying me through the Art Gallery, he changed his programme for the afternoon, and had the kindness to spent the balance of the day with me, showing me through the Houses of Parliament and Westminster Abbey. The tourist should constantly be on the lookout for some suitable companion who is well posted at the place that he proposes to visit. Without such a person to point out things and explain them, one will miss more than he sees. I had just taken leave of a gentleman who had given me considerable assistance, but whose course so differed from my programme, that I was in fear of losing time should I accompany him longer. My new companion was a short-hand reporter of one of the London papers, and thoroughly acquainted in Westminster.

THE HOUSES OF PARLIAMENT.

This is one of the largest buildings ever erected continuously in Europe—perhaps the largest Gothic edifice in the world. It stands upon the bank of the Thames, occupying the site of the old

Royal Palace of Westminster, burnt down in 1834, and covers nearly eight acres. This building has 100 staircases, more than two miles of corridors, and 1,100 apartments! The cost of erection was some $14,000,000, or a little more than that of the Capitol of the United States.

Having procured tickets we entered by the Royal Entrance under the Victoria Tower, one of the most stupendous structures of the kind in the world. It is 340 feet high and seventy-five feet square. The entrance archway is sixty-five feet high, and the vault is a rich and beautiful grained roof of elaborate workmanship, while the interior is decorated with statues of her present Majesty, supported by Justice and Mercy, and the statues of the patron saints of England, Scotland and Ireland.

The first apartment that we entered, was the Robing Room. From this room, after the ceremony of robing, her Majesty on her way to the Throne passes through a magnificent hall 110 feet long, forty-five feet wide and forty-five feet high, called the Victoria Gallery. It contains two magnificent frescoes of events in the history of England, covering large sections of the two side-walls. One represents the death of Nelson, and the other the meeting of Wellington and Blücher after the Battle of Waterloo.

The House of Peers, ninety-seven feet long, forty-five feet wide, and forty-five high, is one of the richest and most magnificent chambers in the world. To the left of the entrance is the Throne on which her Majesty sits when she attends the House, and beside it, the chair of the Prince of Wales. Rich in carvings and lavishly gilt, this noble chamber presents a view of great grandeur.

The subdued light, admitted by the stained glass of its windows, does not dazzle the eye as would a perfect illumination of such giltings, but what is lost in *splendor*, is perhaps gained in *modest grandeur*.

"The arrival of her Majesty is announced within the House by the booming of the cannon. Her entrance is preceeded by the Heralds in their rich dress, and by some of the chief officers of state in their robes. All the peers are in their robes. The Speech is presented to her Majesty by the Lord Chancellor, kneeling, and is read by her Majesty or by him; the Royal Princes and Princesses with the Mistress of the Robes and one of the ladies of the bed-chamber standing by her side on the dais. The return to Buckingham Palace is by three at the latest."

The old custom of examining the cellars underneath the House of Lords, some hours before her Majesty's arrival, is still observed. This custom had its origin in the infamous Gunpowder plot of 1605.

The House of Commons is sixty-two feet long by forty-five feet broad and forty-five feet high; to which England and Wales return 500 members,

Ireland 105, and Scotland 53, making in all 658 members.

St. Stephens Hall 95 feet long, 30 feet wide, and 56 feet high to the apex of the stone groining, is lined by twelve "statues of Parliamentary statesmen who rose to eminence by the eloquence and abilities they displayed in the House of Commons." Fox and Pitt are here placed on opposite sides of the hall, "facing" each other after the manner they were wont to in the House of Commons.

Westminster Hall is 290 feet in length, 68 feet in width, and 110 feet in height. "It is the largest apartment not supported by pillars in the world." Let the reader picture to himself the scenes of the events which history records as having taken place in this venerable Hall. "Here were hung the banners taken from Charles I., at the battle of Naseby; from Charles II. at the battle of Worcester; at Preston and Dunbar; and, somewhat later, those taken at the battle of Blenheim. Here, at the upper end of the Hall, Oliver Cromwell was inaugurated as Lord Protector, sitting in a robe of purple velvet lined with ermine, on a rich cloth of state, with the gold sceptre in one hand, the Bible richly gilt and bossed in the other, and his sword at his side. Here, four years later, at the top of the Hall fronting Palace-yard, his head was set on a pole, with the skulls of Ireton on one side, of Bradshaw on the other. Here, shameless ruffians sought employment as hired witnesses, and walked openly in the Hall with a straw in the shoe to denote their quality; and here the good, the great, the brave, the wise, and the abandoned have been brought to trial. Here (in the Hall of Rufus) Sir William Wallace was tried and condemned; in this very Hall, Sir Thomas More and Protector Sommerset were doomed to the scaffold. Here, in Henry VIII's reign (1517), entered the City apprentices, implicated in the murders on 'Evil May Day' of the aliens settled in London, each with a halter round his neck, and crying 'Mercy, gracious Lord, Mercy,' while Wolsey stood by, and the King, beneath his cloth of state, heard their defense and pronounced their pardon—the prisoners shouting with delight and casting up their halters to the Hall roof, 'so that the King,' as the chroniclers observe, 'might perceive they were none of the descreetest.' Here the notorious Earl and Countess of Somerset were tried in the reign of James I. for the murder of Sir Thomas Overbury. Here, the great Earl of Stafford was condemned; the King being present, and the Commons sitting bareheaded all the time. The *High Court of Justice* which condemned King Charles I. sat in this Hall, the upper part hung with scarlet cloth, and the King sitting underneath, with the Naseby banners suspended above his head. Lilly, the astrologer, who was present, saw the silver top fall from the King's staff, and others heard Lady Fairfax exclaim, when her husband's name was called over,

'He has more wit than to be here.' Here, in the reign of James II., the seven bishops were acquitted. Here Dr. Sacheverel was tried and pronounced guilty by a majority of seventeen. Here the rebel Lords of 1745, Kilmarnock, Balmerino, and Lovat, were heard and condemned. Here, Warren Hastings was tried, and Burke and Sheridan grew eloquent and impassioned, while Senators by birth and election, and the beauty and rank of Great Britain, sat earnest spectators and listeners of the extraordinary scene. The last public trial in the Hall was Lord Melville's in 1806; and the last coronation dinner in the Hall was that of George IV., when, according to the custom maintained for ages, and for the last time probably, the King's champion (Dymocke) rode into the Hall in full armor, and threw down the gauntlet, challenging the world in a King's behalf. Silver plates were laid, on the same occasion, for 334 guests."—*Murray.*

The *Central* or *Octagon Hall* is an elegant and well lighted apartment eighty feet in height. It is covered by a groined roof ornamented with 250 bosses.

The *Clock Tower* is forty feet square and 320 feet high. The Palace Clock in this tower is an eighty-day clock, striking the hours and chiming the quarters upon eight bells. Its four dials on the tower are each thirty feet in diameter.

From the Houses of Parliament we went over to

see Westminster Abbey, which is on the opposite side of the street. The contrast between those buildings is so striking, that old Westminster seemed to be quite an ordinary edifice. As I looked at its weather-beaten and moss-covered walls, and its small proportions as compared with the grand edifice which we had just left; I speculated what the old stable-like building might look like on the inside. We had not entered long before I observed that it was somewhat larger than I had imagined. It is 416 feet long, 203 feet across the transepts, and 101 feet 8 inches to the roof.

Back of the high altar is Edward the Confessor's Chapel containing the graves and monuments of nine kings and queens. In this chapel are the two *Coronation Chairs* upon which all the sovereigns of Great Britain have been crowned since the death of Henry III., (by whom Westminster Abbey was built), beginning with the coronation of his son, Edward I., and Queen Eleanor, October 19th, 1274. One of these chairs has for a seat the venerable stone on which the Scottish kings had been crowned at Scone from time immemorial; but which together with the regalia of Scotland, Edward I. brought with him as trophies in 1296. "This stone is 26 inches long, 16 inches wide, and 11 inches thick."

In the "Poet's Corner" we joined a party and were guided through the chapels.

In Henry VII.'s Chapel we found a very beautiful effigy of the Princess Sophia lying in an alabaster cradle. This infant princess was the daughter of James I., and is not mentioned by some historians, having died at a very tender age.

This chapel contains many royal tombs. Among others are the altar-tomb, with effigy of the mother of Lord Darnley, husband of Mary, Queen of Scots; tomb, with effigy of Queen Elizabeth (her sister, Mary, being buried in the same grave); and the tomb, with a fine effigy of Mary, Queen of Scots, erected by her son, King James IV., of Scotland, (being James I. of England). The face of this image is very beautiful, and generally recognized as a genuine likeness of the Queen. Oliver Cromwell's bones were speedily ejected from this chapel at the Restoration.

In the E. aisle of the North Transept is a remarkable monument to Mr. and Mrs. Nightingale. Death represented in the ghastly form of a sheeted skeleton has just issued from a dark aperture in the lower part of the monument, and aims his dart at the sick lady who has sunk affrighted into her husband's arms. "This dying woman," says Cunningham, "would do honor to any artist."

In another part of the church, we found a fine monument to "Major John Andre, who raised by his merit, at an early period of life, to the rank of Adj. General of the British forces in America, and employed in an important but hazardous enterprise, fell a sacrifice to his zeal and his king and country on the 2nd of October, A. D., 1780, aged29 years, universally beloved and esteemed. His gracious sovereign, King George the Third, has caused this monument to be erected. The remains of Major John Andre were on the 10th of August, 1821, removed from Tappan by James Buchanan, Esq., his Majesty's consul at New York, under instruction from his Royal Highness, the Duke of York, and with the permission of Dean and Chapter finally deposited in a grave contiguous to this monument on the 28th of November, 1821."

There are altogether between twenty-five and thirty kings and queens buried in this Abbey, besides a host of England's most famous statesmen, soldiers, poets and other eminent persons that have flourished within the last five or six centuries, a mere catalogue of whose names would fill whole pages.

It seems odd enough to an American to find large grave-yards in the interior of churches and cathedrals, and to see monuments, tombs and altar-tombs, with the effigies of persons lying in state having all kinds of animals (their crests) lying at their feet; but a day in Westminster will accustom one to such scenes.

ARMS AND CRESTS.

In England, it is very common to place the crests of the nobility with their effigies upon their tombs. Thus Mary, Queen of Scots, has the lion lying at her feet, and in St. Mary's, at Warwick, I learned that the Muzzled Bear is the Earl of Warwick's crest, while the Marquis of Northampton has the Black Swan, and Richard Beauchamp the Bear and Griffin. Even literary characters were not without them, Shakespeare for example, had adopted the Falcon rising argent, supporting a spear, in pale.

SUNDAY IN LONDON.

On Sunday morning, July 18th, I started out at random to find a church where religious service was held. Before going far I came to a large church edifice (St. Pancras) where numbers of people were assembling from all directions and gradually filling up that capacious building which has seats for about 3,000 worshipers. Upon the portico I met the Superintendent of the Mission House, who had accompanied the Vicar of St. Pancras on a visit to Canada, some years ago, and who seemed as much pleased to meet an American as I was benefited by his kind attentions and accommodations. For three-fourths of an hour, he answered me questions and explained the organization of the Church of England, which by the way, is quite as complicated as the organization of the civil government of a nation. Arch-bishops, bishops, vicars, canons, deans, chapters, curates, &c., constitute a list of ecclesiastical dignitaries whose functions are not very easily defined and comprehended by a stranger. Just before service commenced, he conducted me to a seat near the pulpit. Rev. Thorold, the officiating clergyman, is a very able speaker, and made the first attempt at argument in his discourse that I had yet listened to in England. Preaching, in England, like the reciting of prayers, is all so much blank assertion —no more, and no less. I had never before so felt the force of *unquestioned authority* as I learned to feel and appreciate it in the services of the Episcopal Church of England. The very fact of arguing a question is in itself a compromise of its one-sidedness and of the infallibility of the position the preacher may have taken; but let the clergy of an entire nation read the same mass and recite the same prayers in all their congregations, and let them refrain from discussing scriptural texts, and all give one and the same answer to each and every question, and there will soon be an end of sectarianism. The best reasoning has always provoked more doubt than it has established faith, and in consequence, ever been more fruitful of contention than of peace. So long as a people are one-minded they will be peaceful and contended even if they are bound in wretched slavery, but the tide of revolution has set in at London, and the church begins to tremble, and the clergy to argue. In the afternoon, the weather being very fair, I went to

HYDE PARK.

This park has an area of 388 acres, upon which may be seen all the wealth and fashion and splendid equipages of the nobility and gentry of England. A meeting of the Radicals had been an nounced and placarded over the city, inviting al workingmen to be present and enter their protes against Parliament appropriating any money t the Prince of Wales for defraying the expenses o his contemplated trip to India. The novelty o seeing a political meeting on *Sunday*, and that to on the part of the Republicans in monarchial Eng land, was enough to entice me thither, so I wen early and spent an hour with a silver-haired clergy man, upon a settee under the shade of a tree no far from "The Reform Tree," around which, as thi gentleman informed me, the nucleus of Radica meetings is always formed. On my way to th park, I was accompanied for some distance by a certain policeman, (whose acquaintance I hac formed during the week); to him I expressed my surprise at seeing Great Britain compromise th sacredness of the Sabbath with radical Republi canism and Rationalism! "Well," said he, "I we let them have their own way, they will com here and hold their meetings and after they hav listened to their leaders awhile and cheered righ lustily, they will scatter and that is the end of it but when we interfere, there is no telling wher the matter will end. In 1866, we once closed th park against them, and the consequence was a rio in which the police suffered severely from brick bats, and the mob finally took hold of the iron fence and tore it away for a long distance along th park, made their entry, and took their own way." 'Well could you not have punished those offenders according to due process of law?" I asked. "Yes," he rejoined, "we might, but their number was so great that we could never have finished trying them all!" Thus it often happens that what is criminal for one or several to do, goes unpunished when a thousand offend, and besides they open the way to new privileges and greater liberties.

At 3:00 o'clock a mighty flood of the Reform Party, headed by Bradlaugh and Watts, marched into the park and, soon a large meeting of many thousands was formed, which increased in numbers as long as the speakers continued to address them. It is a striking feature of these reform agitations, perhaps of every revolutionary movement that has ever been undertaken and accomplished, that they are headed and lead by men whose personal influence embodies the whole power of the organizations, and whose word and command are their supreme law. This meeting was variously estimated at between 20,000 and 50,000 persons, and this immense concourse of people was as perfectly under the control of Chas. Bradlaugh as the best organized army can be under its general. This harmony must be attributed to the fact that the movement is a spontaneous one in which each member participates because he likes the leader and his principles. It is an encouraging feature of these reformers that they do not despise *everything* that the past has handed down to our time, as th hot-blooded Communists of Paris seemed to be in clined to do in the late *crisis*. The dress of thes agitators speak nothing about bloody revolution as did the "red cap" and slouch hat of the politi cal reformers of Europe of earlier times.

Bradlaugh, for an example, wears a black dres coat, silk dress hat, lay-down collar and blacl necktie, and carries a cane. The great majority o the meeting wore also the fashionable "stove-pipe." These things and the sound judgment of the leader promise "peaceable reforms" but the boundles enthusiasm of the mass of them when inflamator remarks are made, betray the existence of feeling that are akin to pent up volcanoes, and ma break out in violent eruptions when least expected There is certainly fire enough in European Repub licanism to impel them on to mighty efforts wher the proper time comes. The part played by severa ladies in this movement has a salutary influenc for moderation and order. Mrs. Besant and the two daughters of Mr. Bradlaugh are always ac companying him wherever he lectures in London. A table was placed in the center of a circle formed around the leaders, and upon this Mr. Bradlaugh took his stand in addressing the meeting. His voice is far more powerful than that of any other man that I have ever heard, and by the use of medicine which his elder daughter (Alice) reaches up to him very frequently during his speeches, he eeps it perfectly clear to the end; though in these pen air meetings he often stands in the face of),000 to 100,000 persons, speaking by the hour ith a force quite equal to the roaring of a lion. his violent exercise of his vocal organs, he somemes repeats several times every day for a month ı succession, displaying powers of endurance hich are perhaps not equaled by any other living rator. It is an exciting scene to behold acres of ats beclouding the sky while "cheers rend the ir," and to see a field white with hands when votes re taken. Only three persons in this entire meetıg voted in favor of granting the Prince of Wales ıe $700,000 asked for, while some acres of people oted against it.

It should be remembered that this was a meetıg of the *extreme* branch of the Republican party ı London. There is a more moderate party headed y leaders who only despise royalty, but abide with ıe Church and the Christian religion, and which ; said to be far more numerous than the extremists re. In the evening the Radicals had a meeting ı the Hall of Science, where Mr. Bradlaugh adressed them on the subject of religion and social thics. His discourses here are generally very abtruse. None but a very intelligent audience, and ducated in his system of philosophy would undertand his logic or appreciate his wit and humor at ıe expense of royalty and Christianity. The all will hold about 1,500 adults and his congregation (?) is a mixed one comprising both sexes, just like all church organizations; after which, it is a copy. There is no praying, but the Miss Bradlaughs render music upon a melodian or organ both before and after the lecture. In place of the "collection," they charge a small admittance, which becomes a source of considerable revenue; as the hall is crowded at almost every meeting. I must here record one more feature which implies, besides the oratorical powers and progressive originality of the father, an intensity of interest on the part of a daughter, in her father's views, such as is seldom witnessed. Miss Alice B. will, from the beginning to the end of every lecture, keep the eye of her father, watching every change of his countenance from the flush of a glowing enthusiasm to the pallor of bitter contempt, catching every syllable he utters, reflecting with beaming smiles every happy hit he makes, and sinking down to the paleness of utter disdain with him, when he comes to the recital of the heartless oppressions of the aristocracy; continually following his remarks with such an interest as if she was seeing and hearing him for the first time in her life.

I have given a somewhat lengthy account of these Radical meetings and rationalistic sentiments, not on account of their popularity in England, for though hundreds of thousands endorse the movement in London and a number of other cities in Great Britain, still they are by far in the ıinority, at least when the question of religion is ıken; but upon the continent of Europe—in rance, Germany, and I had almost added Switzer- ınd and Italy, the case is already different or fast ecoming so. Rationalism is rampant, and the eader should constantly bear in mind, as I may ot often return to this topic, that the majority of ıe intelligent people in most places are of the amp that I have described as holding these meet- ıgs on Hyde Park and in the Hall of Science in ondon.

Those Radical societies have their own hymn- ooks, and even their children are baptised and ıe dead buried, according to their own forms and eremonies, of unbelief.

Of the numerous other parks in London, I have o room to make mention. Of the British Museum, omprising a collection of books, works of art, an- quities, and curiosities, larger than that of any ther museum contained under one roof in the orld, costing in the aggregate $12,000,000, and he building $5,000,000, and of the South Kensing- on Museum fast approaching the British Museum ı the vastness of its collection, I can only add, hat a complete catalogue of their collections ould fill several large volumes, and to examine ll their contents would require many weeks. here are numerous other museums and galleries f art strewn over the great metropolis, each more omprehensive than the pride and boast of many other cities of pretention in the world, but in London they are only regarded as second rate collections.

If a tourist has only a few days to devote to London, he should not fail to pass through Park Lane (along Hyde Park, at the foot of which lives the son of Arthur, the Duke of Wellington, Commander at Waterloo) thence along Piccadilly, passing Charing Cross, Trafalgar Square, the Strand and Fleet Street, and, having visited Westminster Abbey and St. Paul's Cathedral, will now find

THE TOWER OF LONDON

next in importance. This ancient citadel is the most celebrated in England, and dates back to the time of William the Conqueror (A. D., 1066) at least; but tradition refers it even to Cæsar's time. It covers over twelve acres, and its walls are about three-fifth of a mile in circuit. The outer walls of the White Tower, which stands within the fortifications, are fifteen feet thick.

"This Tower" (The Tower of London) "is a citadel to defend or command the city; a royal palace; a prison of state for the most dangerous offenders; the armory for warlike provisions; the treasury of the ornaments and jewels of the Crown; and general conserver of most of the records of the King's courts of justice at Westminster."—*Stow.*

The Bloody Tower, so called because within it was committed the murder of the princes, Edward V. and Duke of York, sons of Edward IV., by order of Richard III. In this Tower is the Jewel-house containing the regalia and the Crown jewels. Among these, are St. Edward's Crown which was made for the coronation of Charles II., (A. D., 1649), and used in the coronations of all the sovereigns since his time. The Crown made for the coronation of Victoria, consisting of a purple velvet cap enclosed by hoops of silver, and studded with diamonds. It weighs 1¾ pounds. This Crown is estimated at £111,900 (about $550,000). The Crown of the Prince of Wales, of pure gold, unadorned by jewels. The Queen Consort's Crown of gold adorned with precious stones. The Queen's Diadem. Besides, staffs, sceptres, spurs, the Ampulla of the Holy Oil, the Coronation Spoon, the Golden Salt-cellarof State, in the shape of a castle, Baptismal Font, used at the Christening of the Royal Children, a Silver Wine Fountain, maces, swords, bracelets &c.,— all arranged upon a large table, enclosed by a glass case and shielded by iron palings. These treasures are estimated at $17,000,000!

The Horse Armory is contained in a hall 150 feet long and 33 feet wide. In the center, is a line of equestrian figures, 22 in number, clothed in the armor of the various reigns from the time of Edward I. to James II. (1272–1688). When armory had reached its height, just before the introduction of gunpowder, the suits of armor were so heavy and covered the bodies of the soldiers and horses so completely, that a knight in full armor looked much like a turtle sitting upon an armadillo. I saw a suit of armor that weighs 112 pounds, and a spear 18 feet in length. In those days physical strength carried almost everything, while intelligence frequently counted nothing. Looking at those mailed figures makes one almost feel ashamed of his ancestry. Besides one of the blocks upon which were beheaded both the innocent and the guilty in former times, there are also on exhibition the Collar of Torture, 14 pounds in weight, the Thumb-screw, the Stocks, &c., a collection of instruments of torture well calculated to restore in the mind of the beholder, a vivid picture of the dark and wretched past, when man's greatest and most dangerous enemy was his brother. It seemed then to be the best policy of kings, queens, and of all noblemen, to get rid of brothers and sisters at the earliest convenience!

On our way to Beauchamp Tower, the Prison of Anne Boleyn and Lady Jane Grey, we passed Tower Green, where Anne Boleyn, Lady Jane Grey and Catherine Howard, three queens, were beheaded.

This is the place where King Henry VIII. had several of his six wives dispatched, which he could not well have got rid of, by divorce.

I had intended to touch in these remarks a number of other points about London, and especially the almost boundless resources of England's wealthy Lords, but I can only present a single example, and must then hurry on with my account to Continental Europe. The wealthiest nobleman whose home and dwelling-place I passed, is the Duke of Maclew (a Scotchman) whose annual income is estimated at £350,000 or about $1,700,000. He lives at White Hall, near Westminster Bridge.

CHAPTER VII.

LONDON TO PARIS.

On Wednesday, July 21st, the eighth day of my stay in London, I went to Charing Cross Station and procured a ticket for Paris. Before leaving, however, I exchanged my English currency for French money. The rate of Exchange is 25 francs for one sovereign. The exchange clerk explained to me the relative values of the French coins which I found to be much easier to understand than English money.

The table runs thus: 100 centimes equal one franc; and 20 francs, one napoleon. The coins are napoleons, (20f.), 10 franc and 5 franc pieces in gold; francs and half-franc coins in silver; and 10 centime, 5 centime, (the sou), and 1 centime copper and nickle coins, though the centime is not in general circulation now, being equal to but one-fifth of a cent in our money. It was a great consolation to me to know that I would understand the French money perfectly, especially as I expected not to be able to speak with anybody in Paris, except, now and then, with a stray German or Englishman. Soon after entering the train at Charing Cross I met a Frenchman (Prof. P. Simond) who could speak English fluently, having occupied his time in England in teaching French, and was on his way to Paris to spend his vacation there. He offered at once, very kindly, to assist me in Paris, and I felt from that moment that I should be tenfold luckier in making my entry into Paris than I had thus far had reason to expect. The train left London at 6:35 p. m., and was to make connection with a steamer for Calais, (pron. Kăl'ĭ'), thence by rail to Paris, reaching the latter place the next afternoon. The "through ticket" 3rd Class, from London to Paris, cost 21 shillings. Distance 262 miles.

Soon after leaving London, I discovered that I was surrounded by the family of an English merchant, who, having retired from business, had taken his wife and daughters to make a trip to the Continent, with a view to see France and Germany. The mother expressed great delight on learning that I was an American, remarking that "Americans are not so *stiff* in their intercourse." It was not long before I felt that I was in a fair position to spend the *day and night en route from London to Paris* pleasantly, even if we were to be confined to the cars and the boat with the exception of a few hours.

We crossed the Strait of Dover at about midnight, though not *unawares!*

As I had no fears of getting sea-sick upon the Strait of Dover, I took my seat on the deck in confidence of a pleasant voyage. Mrs. L. soon asked me whether I did not expect to get sick, stating that she was in great fear of it. I replied that I hoped our passage was too short for getting sick, as the waves were not apt to rise very high in such a narrow strait. But I was mistaken; the sick were soon moaning in every direction. My gay companions all disappeared except the old gentleman and his younger daughter. A large steamship of 3,000 tons burden would probably show more dignity, but the little steamer upon which we had taken passage, was as fiercely knocked about by the waves, and made fully as much ado about it, as the old "Manhattan" ever did in the middle of the Atlantic. The young lady was keeping close to her father and had already ceased to laugh, when I asked him the last time about their health. *He* was well, but the young lady was also becoming dizzy from the rocking, and turning pale at the terrors of the sea. I hastened to the cabin below and sought relief in lying down. Being both weary and giddy I soon fell into a sleep, from which I did not wake until we reached Calais.

The train for Paris was not to leave until the next morning, so I tried to find rest and sleep in the Waiting Room, but without success. By and by a gentleman came round and offered to conduct us to lodging places. I followed him into the city, through strange streets into a strange house, and was shown to retire in a strange room. Everything seemed in its place, however, so that I had no ocıasion for feeling uneasy. The next morning I ·ose at break of day and took a long walk through he city of Calais, to look about and see as much s possible before I had to leave. This was my irst walk on the Continent of Europe.

I looked about where I might get breakfast, but ıs most of the business houses were not yet open, [stood a poor chance. Into the saloons I would not go, as I could not have asked for what I wanted on account of my inability to speak French; my only hope, therefore, was to find a shop or store that displayed in the window what I wanted, so that I could make my purchase by gestures. I had provided myself with a Conversational Guide Book, in London, containing the French, Italian and German equivalents of English words and phrases most necessary to the tourist; but the French pronunciation is so difficult that I could after all not make myself understood except by pointing out these French words to the shop-keepers. To give the reader an idea of what mistakes an American is apt to make in pronouncing French, I offer the names of two of the most common articles of food. They are *pain* (bread) pronounced pä, and *lait* (milk) pronounced lā. I succeeded, however, later in the morning, when the shops were generally open, to procure a breakfast, whereupon, after having visited a very antique church and examined the strong fortifications of the city, I started for the railway station.

On my way thither I passed the open door of a saloon in which Mr. and Mrs. L., whose friendship I had formed the previous day, sat at coffee. It was a pleasant surprise, and I took my seat with them, drinking coffee for the benefit of the milk (*du lait*) which I poured into it. This done, Mr. L. invited me to accompany him to their hotel to "see what a nice place they had found last night!" It was a excellant hotel, and as we approached the beautiful flower-beds which lined the path leading to the entrance, their daughter came down the walk, and greeted us, the old gentleman remarking that they had been inquiring last night what had become of me. It is very pleasant and agreeable to fall into such society, and to behold the cloth spread and the China and glass ware set with an excellent breakfast (a regular home-fashion scene) after one has spent several hours in lingual conflicts for a breakfast, and seen nothing but the outside of old weather-beaten houses.

I took my seat with the English party and my French friend (Prof. P. S.) in the same car, and left Calais at 7:20 a. m. Everything looked strange again; even more so than when I first came to England. Everybody, except our English company, spoke French, and the cars, the buildings, and the tickets and conductors, seemed all different from what I was accustomed to in England. The houses which we saw from the train, were small and covered with tiles like those which I had seen in northwestern England. We soon passed burial grounds in which the graves were headed with crosses, in place of marble slabs, for tombstones. Large quantities of peat and the white stone quarries in the chalk formations, next arrested our attention. Though it was the 22nd of July, haying was not yet finished. Some of the farmers were, however, engaged in reaping both their wheat and barley. At 8:34 a. m., the English Channel came again into view. Thus we passed along enjoying the scenery of "belle France," (beautiful France), but by and by we became tired of watching landscapes.

To see odd styles of architecture, and watch the strange ways about a people, may afford a pleasant diversion for a time; but the eyes, too, become tired of looking. A striking feature about the agriculture is the smallness of many of the fields; there being no fences, the fields are distinguished by their crops. Some of them are but several rods in extent. The various colors which the different kinds of vegetables assume in their progress of growth and ripening, make the landscape look like an immense expanse of checkered carpet, exceedingly beautiful to behold.

When these scenes seemed no longer to be charming, or we had become too fatigued to appreciate them, we commenced to amuse ourselves in games, joking and tricks, of which the traveler sees and enjoys his fill.

Gambling, which is such a wide-spread social evil in America, is prohibited or restricted to certain fixed days of the year, in some countries of Europe; but games of various kinds are played by the best society, almost everywhere. Notwithstanding all the arguments that may be advanced in favor of games at chess and back-gammon, as exercises in mental gymnastics, and of playing cards as affording pleasant diversion for mixed parties, the diligent tourist, like the industrious student, should not squander much of his time at it.

CHAPTER VIII.

PARIS.

In the middle of the afternoon, we reached the Northern Railway Terminus (*Embarcadere du Nord*) in Paris. This magnificent station covers nearly 10 acres of ground. The arrival and departure sheds in the center are 230 metres long, and 70 metres wide. (The meter is equal to 39.37079 inches). Its facade is 180 metres long, 38 metres (about 125 feet) high and consists of a lofty central arch and two lateral arches. This imposing front is adorned with twenty-three colossal statues of noble female figures, representing the following principal cities of Europe: Paris, (surmounting the central arch), Londres, St. Petersburg, Berlin, Frankfort, Vienne, Bruixelles, Cologne, Amsterdam, Donai, Dunkerque, Boulogne, Compeigne, St. Quentin, Cambrai, Beauvais, Lille, Armiens, Rouen, Arras, Laon, Calais, Valengiens. (1864).

There are a number of other very fine railway stations in Paris, but we can only take room to define their area. The largest is the Strasbourg Railway Terminus, nearly 13 acres in extent; while the Western Railway Terminus covers an area of 5 acres.

As soon as our train had stopped, I followed my French companion (Prof. S.) into the extensive apartments of the station, and passed muster. I expected to be asked for my "passport," but slipped through unchallenged. On passing out into the yard I was again saluted by my English friends who were about entering a "bus" to drive to a hotel. In bidding each other good-by and god-speed on our journeys, I ran a great risk of losing my Parisian friend, in the great multitude of people that thronged the yard and pavement; but fortunately, I found him again in a few minutes.

Before we reached the street, I was already made to feel that some strange scenes and experiences were undoubtedly in store for me in Paris and likely throughout the rest of my continental tour, for I had already observed one of those strange social habits of the Parisians in a most public place which the nice delicacies of our language and customs forbid to describe.

The French, the Italians, and many of the inhabitants of South Germany and parts of Switzerland—I should say all the sunny lands in Europe—have handed down to our day, manners and customs which speak in a language that cannot be misunderstood, and with a force far louder than a whisper, that *it is not very long since man took to dressing himself.* In my intercourse with those people, from Paris to Egypt, I nowhere observed any baneful influences exerted over morality by these practices in question, for they are not thought about by those people which are guilty of them, but many an American will be shocked at them, and go home declaring that such indecencies *must* lead to immoralities, even if they have never gone to the trouble to see whether they actually *do.* Their pernicious influence upon American tastes and manners may be granted, but that does not prove that foreigners, who are cradled, nursed and brought up in these customs, will be affected in like manner. American and English tourists are alike shocked and provoked at the sight of the innumerable nude statues and paintings, on the pleasure gardens and in the art galleries, but the ladies of the continent seem to see as little of indecencies or improprieties in those things, as we do in opening our Bibles and seeing saints and apostles represented with bare feet—the *toes* standing out naked over the sandals, or when we read in the family circle and in the public capacity of teachers and ministers, passages from Scriptures, such as no one would be capable of reading if they were found in a periodical or a newspaper.

During my first month on the continent, I was often vexed to think that much of what I saw, that was not only very interesting and impressive, but which had likewise an important bearing on history, was of such a nature that it would either constitute unfit material for general diffusion, or seem to be incredible to the average reader.

We went down Boulevard (pron. Bool'var') de Magenta about one-third of a mile, to Boulevard de Strasbourg, (pron. Straws'boor'), thence along that avenue (?) to the foot of it (another third of a mile) and continued our walk down Boulevard de Sebastopol to Rue de Rivoli, along which latter street we went half a mile west, where my friend, guide and teacher procured for me a room not far from *his* home.

[With this gentleman I spent from three to five hours daily, during my first stay of fifteen days, in walking about the city seeing sights and studying French reading and pronunciation].

As soon as I had taken my room, I retraced my steps to the railway station and fetched my sachel; this time, alone. It was not a little task, for the distance from my quarters, which were near the center of Paris, to the station, was over two miles. The names of the Boulevards "Magenta, Strasbourg and Sebastopol," I was constantly repeating in my mind, so that I might not forget the way that I had come with my friend, the first time. It was dark by the time I reached my lodging place the second time, but I had seen and learned enough for one day. Almost two miles of *Boulevards* and nearly half a mile of Rue de Rivoli (the finest *Rue* in Paris) thrice walked that afternoon, had presented to me more that was new, than I had expected to see in a week.

THE BOULEVARDS,

like a dozen other of the distinguishing features of Paris, are *new things* to the American; and as they are quite different from anything that I have yet seen of the kind in this country, I shall here take room to note some of their striking characteristics. They are the grandest streets in Paris, sustaining about the same relation to the "Rues" that the avenues in our American cities sustain to the streets. In the French nomenclature, the names applied the different classes of thoroughfares, &c., run as follows: 1st., avenues; 2nd., boulevards; 3rd., rues; 4th., allees or ruelles, and 5th., passages (pron. pahsahjes). In America, the corresponding terms are 1st., avenues; 2nd., ———; 3rd., streets; 4th., alleys, and 5th., passages. It will be observed, that we have here nothing to correspond with the boulevard. In the classification here presented, the term avenue is to designate thoroughfares of great width and shaded with rows of trees on each side, as are the avenues in Washington, D. C. In most American cities, the avenues are diagonal streets or openings connecting distant points of the cities, but this definition loses most of its force when applied to European cities, as they are not built square or rectangular.

Champs Elysees intersects a fine and extensive reservation, (having many of the characteristics of the pleasure garden), extending from the Jardin des Tuileries (Garden of the Tuileries) to the Arc de Triomphe (the Arch of Triumph). Its length is a mile and a quarter, and the garden or park of which it is the grand thoroughfare, is, in one place, about a third of a mile in width. The buildings are consequently a considerable distance off from this carriage-way; but in the boulevards, nothing except the pavement intervenes between the street and the houses. The boulevards of Paris are its widest as well as its noblest streets. The pavements on each side of them, are, in many instances, from twenty-five to thirty feet in width. Thick rows of large and elegant shade-trees border them on both sides, and under these are placed numerous wooden settees for the accommodation of the public. Many of the 6,000 cafes which are strewn over Paris, grace these boulevards with their glass fronts. During the summer season, most of the refreshments and meals are served in front of the cafes on the pavements, and grand is the sight of seeing ten thousand gay Parisians seated along these splendid streets, chattering away over their wine and coffee! Paris is about five miles long by four miles wide, and few are the houses in the entire city that are less than five or six stories high. A few only of the outer streets have as low as four and five story houses. These houses are mostly built of stone, having stone floors, even. Each room is arched over from the four walls; upon these arches are placed the flagstones constituting the next floor, and it is in consequence of this arching that each story is so very high. The white sandstone of the Paris basin constitutes the principal building stone. The city is divided into seven sections, and each section is required by law, to either scrape the fronts of their houses once every seven years, so that the walls look new again, or to paint them anew. No proprietor can choose his time, but when the year is come for his section to repair their houses, it must be done. In consequence of this regulation, the streets never look *checkered* by old and new houses contrasting with each other, but the external appearance of the buildings is made to harmonize, and each street is a unit in appearance. In the finest part of Paris there are few alleys or stables, but splendid rues and boulevards lined with magnificent buildings with elegant fronts, have taken their places. This section is over three miles in length, nearly two in width, and presents scenes of beauty, grandeur and magnificence which are *unrivaled* by anything that the first other cities of the world have ever brought forth.

Its beautiful balconies, as numerous as the windows, constitute another very charming feature of Parisian scenery. The streets are always kept clean and wet by sweepers and sprinklers, and the broad smooth pavements along the boulevards, free from dust and all manner of rubbish or obstructions, afford a suitable promenade for gayety, wealth and fashion to roam. Here beauty's feet may stray, arrayed in the most showy colors or the stateliest attire, without fear of encountering nasty crossings or of being splashed over and soiled by teams upon muddy streets. Ladies attired in gaudy ball-room dresses with long trails, would scarcely present a contrast in dress with the average promenaders. All dress equally well, on Sundays, and on week-days, so that Paris presents to the foreigner, the appearance of a city celebrating an eternal Sabbath. Even when it rains, the pedestrian can walk *for miles* about the city, without being in want of an umbrella. In that event he need only confine his course to the

ARCADES AND PASSAGES.

Webster defines an arcade as "A long, arched building or gallery lined on each side with shops." May the reader not be misled by this definition; for the arcades of Paris do not have shops on *both* sides. They are a uniform system of porticoes generally from twenty to thirty feet in width. Those on Rue de Rivoli are about a mile in length, and the houses to which they belong have been exempted from taxes for thirty years. From these ramify numerous passages and other arcades, connecting different parts of the city.

A "Passage" (pron. pä-sahj) is a street covered with a glass roof, elegantly paved, animals and vehicles excluded or shut off, and lined by the first-class shops in the city. The most remarkable are the Passages des Panoramas, Jouffroy, Verdean, Vivienne, Colbert, Choiseul, Delorine du Saumon, &c. The first of these are the most brilliant and are perhaps not excelled or even equaled by any other in the world, with the solitary exception of Passage des Victor Emanuel of Milan, in Italy. Some of these passages are called

GALLERIES.

The Galerie d'Orleans in Palais Royal, is a good example. This lofty hall, forty feet wide and 300 feet long, extending between a double range of shops, connects the arcades extending around the other three sides of the inner court of that palace, (now turned into shops, bazaars, etc.)

Many of the grand boulevards and rues of Paris have been built since 1848, and the work of widening and improving old streets and building new ones is still going on with constantly increasing vigor.

There are now in progress of construction, broad boulevards, which can only be constructed at the sacrifice of many acres of some of the finest buildings in Paris; but only beauty and grandeur are regarded anything in this noble city, expenses being but little estimated. Notwithstanding the lavish expenditure of money upon this class of improvements, Paris is, of all cities, perhaps the most prosperous on the globe.

Of the wide-spread destruction of public buildings, occasioned by the late war and the stormy days of the Commune, there are but few marks remaining. The Palace of the Tuileries, Hotel de Ville, and a few other buildings, lie still in ruins; but the thirty or more churches which were either greatly damaged or quite demolished, and numerous other public edifices that have been destroyed, have already been restored—some of them with increased magnificence. Besides this, the French have almost finished paying their immense war-debt, while America, whose war ended seven years before theirs, is obliged to sail into the centennial year, still heavily freighted with the obnoxious burden.

Did heaven ever smile upon a more blessed city than Paris? To give the reader an idea of how buildings are torn down to make room for the purpose of extending fine streets, let us refer to the statistics concerning Rue de Rivoli. This street cost $30,000,000. It is two miles in length, and its establishment caused the demolition of upwards of one thousand houses! Thirty millions of dollars, enough to pay for a tract of land that is twenty miles long and eleven miles wide, bought at the rate of $200 per acre; and all this expended on the improvement of two miles of road!

In the Old World, a strip of three to five or six story houses, several hundred feet wide and a quarter of a mile to upwards of a mile in length, is torn down with as much complacent indifference concerning the destruction, as men manifest in mowing so much grass!

As among the most fashionable places in Paris, may be mentioned, Boulevard des Italiens, Palais Royal, Champs Elysees, Jardin des Tuileries and other pleasure gardens and public squares. Boulevard des Italiens, in fair weather, is densely crowded with ladies and gentlemen seated on chairs hired for two to three sous (cents) each. The city clears over $7,000 a year from this source of revenue. But several hundred steps toward the west of this street stand the Académie de Musique (the most splendid opera-house in the world) and the Grand Hotel—two of the most brilliant edifices in the city.

PALAIS ROYAL,

as it now stands, was completed in 1786. This building, like most of the palaces in Europe, is built around a quadrangle, and its plan may be compared to a pupil's slate used for ciphering. The frame corresponds to the form or ground-plan of the buildings, and the slate, to the court or yard which they inclose. This inner court or garden, 700 feet long and 300 feet wide, containing nearly five acres of land, is planted with lime (linden?) trees from end to end, and two flower gardens. In the middle is a fine *jet d'eau* (a fountain). "The garden was thus arranged in 1799; it contains bronze copies of Diane a la Biche of the Louvre, and the Apollo Belvedere; two modern statues in white marble, one of a young man about to bathe, by d'Espercieux; the other of a boy struggling with a goat, by Lemoine; Ulysses on the sea-shore, by Bra; and Eurydice stung by the snake, by Nanteuil, a fine copy in bronze, but more fitted for a gallery than the place it now occupies. Near this statue is a *solar cannon*, which is fired by the sun when it reaches the meridian, and regulates the clocks of Palais Royal."

From the privilege of supplying refreshments and from the hiring of chairs, the Government derives an annual rent of $7,000.

The shops under the arcades are chiefly devoted to articles of luxury, and are among the most elegant in Paris. Many restaurants are on the first floor; here, were formerly the gambling-houses which rendered this place so notorious. The best time for visiting Palais Royal is in the evening, when the garden and arcades are brilliantly illuminated and full of people. The shops of the watch-makers and the diamond windows are then particularly brilliant. In the most magnificent windows the articles have no price marks; but in the best windows in which the articles have price marks, I saw lockets priced $200; rings for $900; ear-rings for $1,000 a pair; a pair of diamond studs for $2,800; crosses for $820; and a necklace worth $3,000.

Palais Royal has been called the capital of Paris. During the early part of the first Revolution, its gardens became the resort of the most violent politicians; here, the tri-coloured cockade was first adopted, and the popular party decided on many of its bolder measures.

There is little room for doubt, that the Cafe, one

of the characteristic features of French society, is a potent factor in civilizing and refining the human race, in these latter times. Religion and intelligence—moral ideas, moral habits and the collective knowledge of our ancentors—has been transmitted from one generation to another down to our time, by the Church and the Schools, principally. But the affairs of the human race have taken a new turn since the invention of printing, by which the steady development of traditional ideas has been arrested, so that the propriety of retaining the standards of ancient civilization as patterns for the present, is being questioned and discussed everywhere. In this great revolutionary era, the authority of the past and even the respect naturally due to parents is very generally disregarded. This latter sad feature of failing to do homage to the aged, is not more the result of a lack of love and esteem, on the part of children for their parents, than of the want of confidence which parents have in themselves. We can take an illustration from our young ladies. A few generations ago, the traditional white cap constituted the head-dress of the young maidens among the catechumens, when they presented themselves for the first time at the altar; now, in place of having all the heads look alike, every head must present a different phase. We still find sections in the Old World, where all the dresses of the young are " cut out of the same piece," so to say, and made after the same pattern, so that all the individuals of a company are almost as nearly dressed alike, as soldiers in uniform. Rev. Bausman, in his Wayside Gleanings, page 141, in describing the appearance of people at church in a certain section of Germany, portrays one feature in these words: "Very pleasant was it to see every lady, old and young, having her hymn book carefully folded in her white handkerchief." The clergy, and the monks and nuns in Europe display like uniformity in their dress. In every old picture or painting, representing a group or company of persons, it will be observed that all the individuals are dressed and combed after the same fashion.

This incessant yearning and seeking for something new is of recent date, and the key-note of a universal system of revolutions. Every season brings a new style of dress, and what is true of fashion is true of everything else. As it would ill become mothers to leave their family for a time and learn the milliners' trade, she makes choice of one of her daughters to be educated in that trade. This young girl after she has learned dressmaking takes the place of the mother in the matter of providing clothes for the family, and becomes in a large measure the mistress of the house. The same thing happens to the baking department of the family. A score of new kinds of pies and cakes have become fashionable in our day, and it is the daughters that have the greatest opportunity to earn this baking of pastries the quickest. The consequence is that the mother soon turns out to be only *second rate cook!* Fully aware that she can neither cook nor make dresses, she resigns her position as head of these departments, respectively o her daughters, who, when once master of the culinary and millinery affairs, will soon be master of the balance of the household affairs. Need I say that the fathers of this generation are served about the same way by their sons? And it is the same between the teacher and the pupil. "Old fogy teacher" or "he has the old ways yet" are expressions that are too common to require any explanation. Happily, most old teachers have cleared the turf, and yielded their laurals to a host of youngsters, ranging in age from about sixteen to twenty years! Thus all difficulties are surmounted in this line, and "Young America" has the reins to himself! Look at the improvements that have resulted from the efforts of inventive genius, and at the progress that the arts and sciences have made. We are in a *new world*, so different from that of our forefathers, that their experiences count almost nothing in this new era. It is a sad picture to see the young and the inexperienced thus groping in the dark, but it is the inevitable consequence of the new turn that things have taken since the inauguration of the *age of reason* [dating from the introduction of printing (?)]. Nevertheless, the young would display much greater prudence, if they would bring many of their schemes and purposes to a lower temperature by sitting still when age rises to speak, and were they to take heed of the counsels and admonitions of those who are older than themselves.

This radical change in the affairs of the world being recognized, it becomes apparent how the power and influence of the Church and Schools must abate in a measure, and give scope, for a season, to a class of institutions more fitted for revolutionary times.. This transition era will likely be marked as a glacial period in the history of religion, during which time rationalism and infidelity will possibly be rampant in Europe, if indeed they do not even establish their dominion in America. But we may hope for a calm after the storm, when things will be steadied down again to a smooth and even flow. In this our time, the transition era, theaters, operas, cafes and the printing press, will play a very important part; the press for the literary public in general, the theaters and operas for the social benefit of the upper class and the cafe for the middle and *large class*, the class which give shape and character to the predominant methods of social evolution. The first cafe in Paris was established in 1697 by an Armenian, and like the establishment of the Hippodrome in New York by Barnum, was a success from the beginning. These institutions increased rapidly in number under Louis XV., and became the favorite resort f distinguished individuals. At present, they bound in every quarter, and justly rank among ıe most remarkable features of the city, being very enerally decorated with unrivaled costliness and plendor. Besides coffee, wine, beer and other re-'eshments, they frequently provide breakfast, and ıany of them also dinners and suppers. In 1874, here were over 6,000 cafes in Paris, doing business ɔ the amount of $24,000,000 annually, or an verage income of $4,000 to each establishment! 'he furniture of the cafe and the plan of conduct-ıg its business resembles that of our fashionable ce-cream saloons more than any other establish-nent that we are acquainted with. The halls are urnished with little tables or marble-stands sur-ounded by chairs or costly sofas, and every person hat enters, is expected to order some kind of drink r refreshment as soon as he has taken his seat. 3oth sexes frequent them alike, and a grand sight t is to see a brilliant company of ladies and gentle-nen sitting in groups and couples about these ;eorgeously decorated halls, enjoying their wine ınd each other's company, thus presenting scenes f gayety and festive pleasure that are seldom out-'ied, even in the ball-room and the opera in this :ountry. A band of musicians render music from ın elevated platform all evening, and an open space n front of the platform is provided for the accom-nodation of those who delight in the dance. The waiting girls of these cafes are usually ladies of remarkable beauty and refinement, whose elegan dresses, graceful manners and rare accomplishmen in conversation and address, are well in keepin with the charming brilliancy of the hall, and th merry and refined company around them.

It is astonishing how cheap these splendid ac commodations of the cafe, almost princely in thei style, can be rendered. A person may enter a caf early in the evening, sit down with his friends and acquaintances, order a glass of wine or beer and enjoy the best music and the pleasures of the most refined society for an hour or two, and when he leaves, his purse is only from three to eight cents the poorer for it. A gentleman may take a lady to the cafe *five* evenings in a week, for between thirty cents and a dollar. He may spent twice as much or even ten or fifty times as much, if he wishes to spend his time in a building whose very window sashes and external ornamentations glitter with gold; but such a lavish expenditure of money is not *required* to be comfortable and happy. These cafes are very orderly houses. It is not fashionable to consume a glass of wine or beer in less than half an hour, and many drink the whole evening at one glass. No one can get drunk at this rate, and any one who would drink fast and should become wild, he would not be tolerated in the cafe, as no lady would remain in his society.

There are some fast drinking-houses even in Paris, and more in some sections of Germany, but ven those sent few or no drunk men upon the treets. A fellow that would stagger upon the pavement would be conducted to the station house at nce. I did not see a single drunk person in Paris n half a month's stay, and only several in the rest f my tour through Europe. It is an encouraging ign of the times, that the cafe is being introduced n America. May it soon take the place of our ambling-halls and drinking-hells. See what Macaulay says of the Cafe, as he is quoted by Webter in his Unabridged Dictionary under the word Coffee-house.

CHAMPS ELYSEES,

Champs Elysees, (pron. Shangs-ai-le-zai), a term quivalent to "The Elysian Fields" of the Greeks, s perhaps the most charming place in the world. t is a paradise in reality, as its names implies; nd during the summer evenings, when its many housand gas jets blaze in globes of various colors, and the magnificent illuminations of its grand cafes produce a brilliancy of coloured light intense enough to see pins on its walks and flower-beds, he scenes become grand beyond description. Immense throngs of people gather around the cafes in he evening to see the youths and beauties whirl n the mazy dance, and listen to the bewitching trains of the sweet music there rendered. It is not a rare thing to see spectators go into raptures on these occasions, for I have seen few places where nature and art so harmonize and unite in producing scenes of enchanting beauty and creating fee ings of ecstatic delight, as here on Champs Elysee The atmosphere of Paris, too, is preëminently so and balmy, and the temperature so even that ladi may sit in the most brilliant attire all evening i the open air under the trees of this pleasure-garde without the least danger of contracting a cold. On of the first evenings that I enjoyed these scenes o indescribable beauty, I could not help but observ to my companion, that the finest poetical descrip tions of a celestial Paradise, were not ideal repre sentations of imaginary pleasures, but true word images of the joys and beauties of the "Elysia Fields" (Champs Elysees) in Paris.

The buildings which front upon this lovely plac are among the most elegant in the city, bein finely painted, even on the outside, like those i the boulevards. I saw one, whose balconies wer all gilt, from the bottom to the attic story, remind ing one of the splendor of the foremost royal man sions.

Palais de l'Elysee, lies contiguous to this plac and gave origin to its name. It was a favorite resi dence of Napoleon I. When he returned from Elba, he occupied it until after the defeat of Water loo. It was also the official residence of Napoleon III. while he was President of the French Repub lic. At present it is occupied by Marshal Mac Mahon during the recesses of the National As sembly.

In about the center of Champs Elysees, is the Palais de l'Industrie, the great Exhibition Buildings, in which the World's Fair was held in 1855.

The Avenue des Champs Elysees intersects Champs Elysees, and is a mile and a quarter in length. Its foot-pavements are twelve feet wide. This is the favorite walk of the gay Parisians.

"On sunny winter-days, or cool summer-evenings numerous parties of all classes are seen, enjoying the lively spectacle before them, seated on iron chairs hired for three or four sous, (cents), or on the wooden benches placed at intervals on the sides of the avenue, while elegant carriages roll in procession along the road." — *Galignani's Paris Guide.*

Place de la Concorde, called Place de la Revolution in 1792, (when the guillotine was erected here), is at the east end of Champs Elysees, adjoining the Jardin des Tuileries. The square is enclosed with balustrades, upon which stand eight colossal statues of the chief provincial cities. In the center of it stands the Obelish of Luxor. This magnificent monument of ancient Egypt, was brought to Paris in 1833 and erected in 1836. It weighs 250 tons, and to transport it from Thebes to the place where it now stands required three years. It is one of two monoliths that stood in front of the great temple of Thebes, where they were erected 1550 years before Christ. Both of them were given to the French Government, by Mehemet Ali, Viceroy of Egypt, " in consideration of advantages conferre(by France on Egypt in aiding to form the arsena and naval establishment of Alexandria." Onl; one was removed. It is 72 feet 3 inches high. It greatest width is 7 feet 6 inches at the base, and feet 4 inches at the top. The pedestal upon whicl it stands, is 15 feet by 9 feet at the bottom and feet at the top, and weighs 120 tons.

The transportation and re-erection of this obelisk cost the French Government about $400,000. A dear present! No wonder that they did not go t(fetch the other one.

Galignani enumerates the following events which occurred here and rendered the Place de la Concorde famous:

" July 12, 1789.—A collision between Prince de Lambesc's regiment and the people became the signal for the destruction of the Bastille.

Jan. 21, 1793.—Louis XVI. suffered death on this place.

From Jan. 21, 1793, to May 3, 1795, more than 2,800 persons were executed here by the guillotine.

Feb. 23, 1848.—The first disturbances that ushered in the memorable revolution of that year took place here.

Feb. 24, 1848.—Flight of Louis Philippe and his family by the western entrance of the Tuileries Garden.

Nov. 4, 1848.—The Constitution of the Republic was solemnly proclaimed here, in the presence of the Constituent Assembly.

Sept. 4, 1870.—The downfall of Napoleon III. and the Third Republic proclaimed, after the disaster of Sedan.

May 22, 1871.—A desperate conflict between the Versailles troops and the Communists, the latter in their retreat setting fire to public and private buildings."

JARDIN DES TUILERIES,

A pleasure-garden over fifty acres in extent (containing flower-beds, an extensive orangery, trees, statues and fountains) intervenes between Place de la Concorde and the Palace of the Tuileries, and, in connection with Champs Elysees, constitutes a continuous garden and park whose total length is over a mile and three quarters.

This magnificent reservation penetrates almost to the heart of the city. Its width is in one place nearly half a mile, being about one fifth of a mile wide at the Tuileries on the east, while it tapers down to about 450 feet (the width of Avenue des Champs Elysees) at the Arch of Triumph on the west end of it. The Avenue des Champs Elysees and the principal avenue in the Tuileries Garden are in a perfectly strait line, so that a person standing in the center of the avenue at the Tuileries will see both sides of the Arch of Triumph, nearly two miles away from him; while the center is concealed from his view by the Obelisk of Luxor standing in the center of Place de la Concorde, as above described. Stepping a few yards to either side throws the obelisk out of the way and affords one a perfect view of that noble arch (one of the most stately monuments in existence). The tourist can not approach that imposing monument called

ARC DE TRIOMPHE DE L'ETOILE

to greater advantage than by this avenue, starting out from the ruins of the Tuileries. As some of the finest scenes and most important places in Paris are met with, by this approach, one should allot a whole day to this walk. He will have half a mile to the obelisk in the center of Place de la Concorde, which, with its surroundings, will require him hours to see. Three thousand feet further, is the Rond Point of Champs Elysees. A quarter of a mile short of this, he will have found the Exhibition Buildings on his left and Palais de l'Elysees on his right. Having seen these, he may make his approach of the Arch of Triumph without further interruption. From Rond Point to the center of the arch, it is about 3,800 feet more. It is only after the visitor comes within half a mile of its base that the monument begins to assume its gigantic proportions. This proud monument was designed by Chalgrin, having been decreed by Napoleon I. in 1806. The work was suspended from 1814 till 1823; labor was resumed then, but it was not completed before 1836. Thus, thirty years of time and over $2,000,000 were bestowed upon the erection of this historic monument, which is perhaps destined to hand down to future generations both the names of the victors and of the numerous vanquished cities that were subject to the authority of Napoleon I. The great central arch is forty-five feet wide and ninety feet high, over which rises a bold entablature and the crowning attic. The transversal arch is twenty-five feet wide and fifty-seven feet high. The total height of the monument being 152 feet; and its breadth and depth 137 feet and 68 feet respectively. The fronts of the structure are towards Champs Elysees and Porte de Neuilly, the city gate near Bois de Boulogne.

The general plan of this imposing monument is borrowed from that of the famous arches at Rome; but the transversal arch is an additional feature, while its reliefs, and inscriptions, and its colossal proportions throw the arches of Rome into comparative insignificance. The interior sides of the piers are inscribed with the names of ninety-six victories; under the transversal arches are the names of generals. A group upon the northern pier of the eastern front represents the departure of the army in 1792:—"The Genius of War summons the nation to arms." The group on the southern front represents the triumph of 1810:—Victory is in the act of crowning Napoleon. History with pencil in hand is about to record his deeds upon a tablet before her; conquered towns are at his feet. Fame surmounts the whole, blowing her bugle of praise. The group on the southern pier of the western front represents the French nation's resistance to the invading army of 1814:—A young man defends his wife, his children and his father; a warrior falls slain from his horse, and the Genius of the Future encourages them to action. Upon the northern pier is represented the peace of 1815:—The warrior sheathes his sword, the farmer has caught a bull with a rope, and is taming him for purposes of agriculture, while a mother with her children is sitting by, and Minerva sheds her protecting influence over them. Every group is 36 feet in height and each figure 18 feet.

A chain fence encircles this proud and noble monument, and shuts off all conveyances. Pedestrians can enter until dusk. An ascent of 272 steps brings the visitor to the platform at the top, from which one of the finest views of Paris and the surrounding country may be enjoyed.

There are three other triumphal arches in Paris. The oldest is that of Porte St. Denis. It was erected by the city of Paris in 1672. The principal arch is 25 feet wide, and 43 feet high; and the total height of the structure is 72 feet. Its reliefs and other representations are superb.

The triumphal arch over Porte St. Martin is 54 feet wide by 54 feet high. The central arch is 15 feet wide by 30 feet in elevation. It was built in 1674, two years after the erection of Porte St. Denis.

The last of the three inferior arches was erected by order of Napoleon in 1806. It has a base of 60 feet by 20 feet, and is 45 feet high. The cost of erection was about $275,000. It stands near the Tuileries at the Place du Carrousel, after which it was named, and which was so called from a great tournament held by Louis XIV. in 1662. The entablature is supported by eight Corinthian columns of marble, with bases and capitals of bronze, adorned with eagles. The attic of this arch is surmounted by a figure of Victory in a triumphal car with four bronze horses hitched to it. These were modelled by Bosio from the celebrated historic horses which Napoleon brought from Venice to Paris in 1797, but which were restored by the allies in 1815, and now stand again in the Piazza of St. Mark at Venice, as they had since 1205. The original (those in Venice) are gilt, but those in Paris are black.

THE TOMB OF NAPOLEON I.

The tomb and last burial place of the great Napoleon, which is in Eglise des Invalids, is perhaps the most imposing monument of the kind in the world. I have not found its equal anywhere; nor anything to rival it even, in costliness and splendor, except those of several of the Popes at Rome. The tomb which covers the sarcophagus into which the mortal remains of Napoleon I. brought from St. Helena, were placed April 2nd, 1861, consists of a immense monolith of porphyry weighing 67 tons, brought from Lake Onega in Russia at an expense of $28,000. This tomb, 13½ feet in height, stands in the center of a circular crypt, and is surrounded by twelve colossal statues representing so many victories. The pavement of the crypt contains a crown of laurels in mosaic, and a black circle upon which are inscribed the names of the following victories: Rivoli, Pyramids, Marengo, Austerlitz, Iena, Friedland, Wagram and Moskowa. A large bouquet of immortelles (everlasting flowers) lying upon the tomb is emblamatic of the immoritality of the great soldier's fame. Over the bronze door which leads to the crypt, are inscribed the following words, quoted from the Emporor's will:

"Je desire que mes cendres reposent sur les bordes de la Seine, au milieu de ce peuple Francais que j'ai tant aime."

"I wish my remains to be laid on the banks of the Seine, amongst that French people whom I have loved so much."—*P. Simond.*

In the center of an adjoining chapel, stands the tomb of Joseph, King of Spain, the eldest brother of Napoleon I. His mortal remains were brought hither in 1864.

The dome which rises over the tomb of Napoleon I. is one of the proudest monuments in Paris, and its gilt and glittering cupola may be seen many miles around. The cross on top of the globe and spire surmounting this dome is 323 feet above the pavement. Leaving Eglise des Invalids from the southern entrance, which leads to the tomb of Napoleon I., a spectacle presents itself to the beholder in the form of a grand fountain throwing its water high into the air. It is at

THE ARTESIAN WELL OF GRENELLE.

M. Mulot commenced to bore at this well in 1834, but did not succeed in reaching water until February 26th, 1841, by which time his boring instrument had reached the depth of 1,800 feet, and the water suddenly gushed forth with tremendous force. The whole depth is lined by a galvanized iron tube that is 21 inches in diameter at the top and 7 inches at the bottom. The amount of water yielded every 24 hours is 170,940 gallons. Its temperature is about 82 degrees Fahrenheit.

Twenty years after the sinking of this well, that is in 1861,

THE ARTESIAN WELL OF PASSY,

near the Arch of Triumph, was completed. This yielded at first 5,000,000 gallons in 24 hours; it yields now over 3,000,000 gallons per day. A third artesian well is in Boulevard de la Gare.

There are, besides these artesian wells, 35 monumental fountains, 88 plain fountains and over 2,000 water-plugs in the city.

NOTRE DAME.

The Cathedral Church of Notre Dame is the grandest church of the rose-window class that I met with in my whole tour of Europe. The length of this edifice is 390 feet, and its greatest width at the transepts 144 feet. It is said to be capable of holding 21,000 persons. The nave is 225 feet long,

39 feet wide and 102 feet in height to the vaulting; the windows are 36 feet high. Its two western towers are each 204 feet high, and the spire about 270 feet. The first thing that arrests the attention of the visitor on approaching it, are the grotesque figures of its antique gargoyles, several hundred in all, which give the church a very odd appearance. The three portals (at the west end) contain about 300 images. Its organ is 36 feet broad, 45 feet high and contains 3,484 pipes. But among the most remarkable features of this magnificent cathedral are its splendid rose-windows, representing a variety of scripture and legendary subjects, and its choir and sacristy. Here, are mitres and crosses glittering with jewels, and the church-utensils and vestments. The most gorgeous are the robes worn by Pius VII. at the coronation of Napoleon I., and several series of brilliant robes profusely embroidered in silver and gold. It seems that the place upon which Notre Dame now stands, was first occupied by a heathen temple erected in the time of the Romans; for, among nine large stones dug up in 1711, one bears the effigy of the Gallic deity Hesus, and the other was a votive altar raised to Jove.

THE PANTHEON.

About half a mile distant from the island of the Seine upon which Notre Dame stands, on an eminence south of the river, is located the Pantheon, or church of St. Genevieve. This building cost

$6,000,000. The six fluted columns of its portico are 6 feet in diameter and 60 feet high. The whole number of Corinthian columns in and about this superb edifice is 258. The arched ceilings of the interior are 80 feet high. The dome is 66 feet in diameter and its height from the pavement to the top is 268 feet. I have seen no other dome in Europe that resembles so closely the dome on the Capitol of the United States, both on account of its fine illumination by natural light, and in its general design. One section of the frescoes in the canopy of the dome on our national capitol, represents the deification of Washington. In the dome of the Pantheon at Paris, Clovis, Charlemagne, St. Louis and Louis XVIII., are represented as rendering homage to Ste. Genevieve, who descends towards them on clouds, and Glory embraces Napoleon. In the heavenly regions are represented, Louis XVI. and Marie Antoinette, Louis XVII. and Madame Elizabeth.

In 1791, Mirabeau was interred here with great pomp, and in the same year took place, the celebrated apotheoses (deifications) of Voltaire and Rousseau. The remains of Mirabeau and of Marat were afterwards depantheonized, and the body of the latter was thrown into a common sewer.

The vaults are under the western nave. In these the "monuments and funeral urns are arranged like the Roman tombs in Pompeii." There are two concentric passages in the center, where small sounds are repeated by loud echoes. A hand holding a torch issues from one side of Rousseau's tomb, meaning that he is a light to the world even after death.

LA MADELEINE

is the third and the last of the large churches of Paris to which I can direct particular attention. It is 328 feet long by 138 feet wide, covering over an acre of ground, and its erection cost over $2,500,000. This structure was commenced in 1764, but the work was suspended during the revolution of 1789. Napoleon had once directed Vignon to complete it for a Temple of Glory, but Louis XVIII. restored it to its original destination in 1815. It is approached at each end by a flight of 28 steps, (the same number that constitute the Scala Sancta at Rome), extending along the whole length of the facade; and a Corinthian colonnade of 52 columns, each 49 feet high and five feet in diameter, surrounds it on every side.

There are scores of other churches in Paris that are interesting on account of the various styles of architecture which they represent, but I will only make mention of one more, and that on account of its terrible historical associations. It is the church of St. Germain l'auxerrois (pron. sang jer-mang lo-zher-wa). It was from the belfry of this church, that the signal was given for the commencement of the Massacre of St. Bartholomew, August 23rd, 1572. Its bells tolled during the whole of that dreadful night. This church was the theater of another outbreak on the 13th of February, 1831, when everything within the church was destroyed.

THE LOUVRE.

The reader may form an idea of the extent of these buildings, when he reflects that the space covered and inclosed by the Old and New Louvre and the Tuileries, is upwards of sixty acres. The court of the louvre is one of the finest in Europe, and its art galleries are among the richest in the world. The Long Gallery alone covers nearly an acre and a quarter, being 42 feet wide and 1,322 feet long! A person can well spend weeks or even months in the museum of the Louvre, but simply to walk through all of its brilliant galleries will require about three hours! I cannot stop to say more than that its collections of paintings and of sculpture is probably much larger than any other in the world.

Besides what I have already described and enumerated, Paris has its Bois de Boulogne containing large botanical and zological gardens, three race courses, the longest nearly two miles in circuit, lakes and drives; also many other gardens, squares, towers, columns, &c.—all full of beauty or interesting on account of the historical events and incidents associated with them; but I must now devote the remainder of my space to the

THEATERS, OPERAS

and other places of amusement of the great capital

of the social world. Places of amusement are the leading feature of Paris, and a boundless variety, adapted to the wants and tastes of every class of society, are strewn in endless profusion all over the city. The concert season lasts almost all the year round, though the highest class are limited to the winter and spring. Masked balls take place throughout the Carnival, in the winter season, and are thus spoken of and described by Galignani: "The most amusing are at the Opera-house, where they begin at midnight and continue till daybreak. No stranger who visits Paris at this season of the year should omit a visit to one of the *Bals masques* at this theater, for it is difficult to imagine a scene more curious and fantastic than that presented in the *Salle* of the Grand Opera at a Carnival Ball. On these nights the pit is boarded over and joins the stage; the vast area of the whole theater forming a ball-room of magnificent proportions, which, brilliantly lighted, and crowded with thousands of gay maskers attired in every variety of colour and costume, forms a sight not easily forgotten. Ladies should not go except as spectators in a box and under the protection of their relatives. The ticket costs $2.00. To witness this scene in perfection the visitor should wait until 12 or 1 o'clock, when the company is completely assembled and the votaries of the dance are in full activity. On entering the vast *salle* at such a moment the effect is scarcely imaginable, the gorgeousness of the immense heater, the glitter of the lights, the brilliancy and variety of the costumes, the enlivening strains of music, the mirth of the browd, and, above all, the the untiring velocity with which the dancers whirl themselves through the mazes of the waltz, polka and mazourka, present an appearance of bewindering gayety not to be described. * * * * On some occasions of special enthusiasm the crowd take up the leader of the orchestra with the most frantic plaudits, and in more than one instance have carried him in triumph round the theater. It is scarcely necessary to add that at these balls the *roue* (profligate) may find an endless variety of pleasant adventures." On some days during the Carnival, crowds of masked persons, exhibiting all sorts of antics, appear in the streets, and people assemble on horseback, in carriages and on foot, to witness the scene.

"The Carnival was prohibited in 1790, and not resumed till Bonaparte was elected first consul." Great was the joy of the Parisians when the Carnival was again restored!

The Opera-house referred to in the extract above quoted, is the Academie Nationale de Musique, or French Opera-house, also sometimes called the new Opera-house. It is generally admitted to be the finest Opera-house in the world. The space covered by this magnificent building is 140 metres by 122, (about 470 feet by 410), or nearly four and a half acres. It has seats for 2,520 spectators. The staircases, walls and ceiling are of the finest marble. The "house" for the spectators or audience is built entirely of stone and iron, rich in decorations and thick with gold. The stage alone is a quarter of an acre in extent, being 128 feet wide by 85 feet long. Below the stage there is a depth of 47 feet, from which the scenes are drawn up all in one piece. This abyss below the stage was obtained at an immense cost, as the architect had to lay the foundations far below a subterranean body of water, but the advantage thus gained enables them to present scenes that are marvelous. "The singers in this opera are pupils of the Conservatoire, and the *corps de ballet* consists of the most distinguished dancers of the day. Great attention is paid to costume and general effect." During the matchless performances of a night that I was present, there were at one time nine large horses and a procession of several hundred actors upon the stage, and it was far from being full. One of the most beautiful and astounding performances of the night was the production of a series of transformations that were as sudden and as astonishing in their developments as is the metamorphosis of the gaudy butterfly from the groveling worm. As the curtain rose there stood upon the stage a mighty fortress, massive and strong. We had seen it but long enough to observe how thick and how rough from age its weather-beaten walls were, when there was heard a crash, and the mighty citadel had fallen out of sight; but there still remained a most beautiful castle which must have been contained inside of the citadel but hid from the view by its towering walls. This castle was beautiful beyond description. It was fairer far than the castles of the kings seem to be, except when "distance lends enchantment to their view." But the second scene was as ephemeral as the first. We beheld its fascinating beauties only a few seconds when its four walls again dropped into the abyss below, and there issued from its inner apartment a host of beautiful little actresses such as I did not see upon any other stage in Europe. These little fairy-like beauties, many perhaps not more than from 5 to 10 years of age, all dressed in the most brilliant costumes, at once skipped into a dance "running the ring and tracing the mazy round," to the great satisfaction of the admiring spectators, who were as much delighted by the gayety, grace and accomplishment which they displayed in their performances, as they have been astonished at their sudden and almost miraculous appearance.

AT A BALL.

Dancing is the favorite amusement in Paris, and these exercises are conducted on a grand scale, even during the summer season. I attended a Public Ball one evening, when almost the entire floor (covering nearly three fourths of an acre) and the adjoining garden of about the same area, were thronged by thousands of gay and jovial dancers, all wild from the excitement produced by the rhythmical motions and music of that playful exercise.

INCIDENTS.

The reader can not be more curious to know how one that is unacquainted with the French language can get along in Paris, than I was when I first took up my residence there. The first morning I went out to seek some place where I might get fresh milk; *Lait* is the French name of it as I found it in my conversational guide book. I soon found that name upon a card of pasteboard hanging at the door of a shop where bread and fruits were displayed in the window. On entering the store a clever Frenchman politely addressed me, but he soon discovered that I was none of the *loquacious* kind, in French. I asked for *lait*, pronouncing the word as if it was spelt l-a-t-e, but he did not understand me. I could adorn my conversation neither with verbs nor with adjectives, so I repeated the word *lait* several times with the rising inflection, by which he readily inferred that I wanted something, though what that something was, remained a mistery to him, all the same. By and by, I pointed out the word lait to him, on seeing which, he exclaimed "—— —— du lā!" and gave me what I wanted. Thereafter I visited him from two to five times every day, according to convenience, to get my "du lā*it!*". Of "du pä*in*" (bread) and smoked sausages, I constantly kept a supply in my satchel, so that when I entered a new city, I could well get along until I had become acquainted. Fruits and a very healthy and nutricious kind of nuts, (the Brazilian nuts), I bought in great abundance and exceedingly cheap from such as hawked them about on the streets. Five to ten centimes (1 to 2 cents) would buy 7 or 8 large Brazilian nuts and 6 to 8 fine juicy pears, or as many delicious plums, of which I was extremely fond. By thus reducing the number and variety of my dishes at the regular meals, I only enhanced the pleasures of the palate instead of reducing them; for he who "does not eat but when he is hungry, nor drink except when he is thirsty," will enjoy the humblest meal much more than the pampered dedauchee can relish the richest feast. As beer does not please my palate, and because the water fountains of Paris were often out of my reach when I was thirsty, I soon took fruit to supply the place of drink, and thus, in Paris already, I laid the foundation of a dietary system that ensured me not only health, happiness and convenience of procuring it alike in all countries, but that proved to be very economical too. For from 40 to 60 cents a day, I supplied all the necessaries, and more of the luxuries of life, than most of us are accustomed to, even in voluptuous America.

CHAPTER IX.

VERSAILLES.

On my voyage across the Atlantic, I had formed the friendship of a young clergyman, (Rev. O.), of New York, who wished to make a summer vacation tour through western Europe, visiting Ireland, Scotland, England, France, Italy, Switzerland and Germany. On comparing programmes, we noticed that he would likely come to Paris during the time that I had alotted to that city. We therefore agreed that each should drop a letter to the other, immediately after reaching Paris, so that he who should happen to come last might at once know where to find the other. One evening, when I came home, the card of Rev. O., my American friend, was handed to me by the landlord, who informed me by his gestures that he had been there to call on me. The card was backed by a note asking me to meet him at No. —, Rue ——— ———. Though that street is perhaps not more than an eighth of a mile long, I soon found it upon my map of Paris, which was a very excellent one, as the maps of all large foreign cities generally are and must be, in order that persons who cannot speak the languages of those cities, may still be able to find any places without asking any one where they are or which way to go. The map of Paris, for example, is divided into numerous squares by arbitrary lines. Those which run vertically down the map are lettered, and those which cross it horizontally are numbered. At the side of the map is a table of all the streets, with references to the squares on the map, designating between what lines they are found, or which they intersect. By the aid of such a map, I started out the next morning to meet my friend, whose quarters were in a distant part of the city, about three miles away. I found him without difficulty. He was accompanied by two gentlemen from London that had come with him to see Paris and its environs. It is both novel and pleasant for two such lonely pilgrims as my New York friend and I were when we left home, to meet each other again in a foreign city, and introduce to each other the friends which one picked up by the way. We soon agreed to go all together to Versailles, the French Capital, that day. This was Tuesday, July 27th. At 10:40 a. m., we crossed the fortifications of Paris, and soon came into view of Bois de Boulogne, the great park of Paris. Five minutes later we crossed the Seine at St. Cloud, a small town, where we stopped to see the ruins occasioned by the siege of Paris in 1870. We had considerable trouble, however, in identifying the strongholds and redoubts held by the Prussians in that memorable siege, as nobody seemed to understand any of our French! On one occasion, Rev. O., while asking a lady for a certain place, called on Mr. K———, one of the Londoners, to come and see whether he could make this woman understand any of *his* French! It was altogether a day of odd adventures and fun. After enjoying the lovely prospects an hour, we walked another hour in great perplexity as to what directions we should take to find a railway station where we might take a train for Versailles, but finally succeeded. We did not understand more from those who directed us, than the direction we should take, never knowing the distance. It is more than a joke, for a party to be obliged to walk several miles for a station, when they had expected to reach it in a quarter or half a mile at most! When we arrived at the station at Sevres, our difficulties only commenced. "When will the next train leave for Versailles, and where can we procure our tickets?" were questions which engaged our best energies and all our ingenuity for half an hour, besides a rash adventure on my part, before they were solved. (It seems to me now, that throughout my tour, I always got into more trouble when I had company to rely upon, than when I was alone). By means of motions with our hands and by pronouncing the name Versailles, we made them understand where we intended to go to; but when we asked for "billets," they did not offer us any. They showed us, however, that the train was due at 1:10, by pointing out those figures on the dial of the clock. About 15 minutes before the train was due, we asked again for tickets, and when they were again refused, we began to fear that the tickets had to be procured on the opposite side of the railroad. We therefore crossed by a foot-bridge near the station, but could not approach the house on the other side, on account of the high fence which shut every body off from the tracks. When our plans were thus frustrated our company became alarmed with the fear that we might miss the train for want of tickets, and fail to see Versailles that day. At this crisis I ascended the bridge and climed down along the walls on the inside of the fence; suspending myself from the lowest iron bars along the bridge, I thus dropped myself into the yard below! But our discouragement reached its climax, when I found that the door was closed and locked, which we had hoped was the ticket office. I could not get out of that inclosure, as the fences were high, the gates locked and the bridge from which I had dropped myself, was out of my reach. Several railroad men saw me immediately, who appeared as much astonished at my coming into that place, as I was perplexed in my awkward position. I did not misinterpret their French this time, however, for the way they looked up toward the sky, and their gestures and chattering, plainly indicated that they wondered where I came from. I motioned them that I came "from above," and pointed toward the bridge. What fine or punishment might have been inflicted for my intrusion I do not know, but I was only rebuked in language which I did not understand, and sent out through one of the office doors which they unlocked for the purpose. My companions were now in great glee at this termination of my adventure, one of them observing that I might soon be landed in *close quarters*, at my present rate of progress! I responded that we were a party corporate, and that three fourths of what any one did was to the credit of the other three. The train soon came, and we took our places on the top of the cars and rode on to Versailles. This was the only ride I had in two-story railway cars, but our trip was such a delightful one in the second story of those cars, that I often wished for like accommodations again.

The National Assembly was in session when we reached Versailles, but we could not gain admittance. We immediately went to the Palace, which is devoted to the reception of a rich and splendid historical museum unparalleled in Europe. There are altogether some 34 salles or galleries, which require upwards of an hour to walk through. The paintings are arranged chronologically, and it is this classification, as well as the magnitude of the collection, that render the museum one of the most famous in Europe. Adjoining this palace, are the gardens and park, upon the establishment and improvement of which, Louis XIV., (1616) spent $200,000,000! This immense sum would pay a tract of land 100 miles long and 10 miles wide, bought at $300 per acre! Many millions have since been spent upon it. It is at the present day one of the finest pleasure-gardens in Europe. Its fountains are among the most magnificent in existence. These are made to play only once (the first Sunday) every month; to supply the water in sufficient aboundance for this magnificent display, costs on each occasion $2,000! It is a source of the purest happiness for a party of Republicans, as ours was, to see the very palace and gardens which Napoleon III. once occupied as a royal mansion, now held as the common property and the peaceful promenade of the pleasure-seeking masses. How changed the scene! That which was prepaired for the king, is now enjoyed by the common people. Such are the fruits of the French Republic, which has now broken the fetters of royalty for the third time.

On Sunday, August 1st., I visited this garden and park again, this time to see the fountains play. It is impossible to do justice to this pleasure-garden even in two days. In the center is the grand canal 186 feet wide and nearly a mile long, intersected at right angles by another canal that is 3,000 feet long. My rambles were confined to the section intervening between the palace and the Bassin d'Apollon, which is at the nearer end of the Grand Canal. The fountains and jets in this section, north and south of the Allee du Tapis Vert (green lawn), are almost innumerable. They do not all play at the same time, so the crowd can follow them from basin to basin until Neptune with his numerous jets, the last and the greatest of them all, is reached. The Terrasse du Chateau with Silenus, Antinous, Apollo and Bacchus, after the antique, lies next to the palace. Immediately below is the Parterre d'Eau, upon whose border repose twenty-four magnificent groups in bronze, namely, eight groups of children, eight nymphs and the four principal rivers of France, with their tributaries. Toward the left of this lies the Parterre du Midi, and still further south, along the palace, lies the Orangerie. A flight of 103 steps lead down to an iron gate on the road to Brest.

Parterre de Latone lies in advance of Parterre d'Eau, which two paterres (pits) the Allee du Tapis Vert (green carpet) and the Grand Canal, lie in a straight line and present a charming view nearly a mile and a quarter in length. Bassin Latone is surrounded by a semi-circular terrace crowned with yew-trees and a range of statues and groups in marble. (It would require the space of a volume to describe all the fine statuary of this garden). This fountain consists of five circular basins rising one above the other in the form of a pyramid, surmounted by a group of Latona with Apollo and Diana. "The goddess implores the vengeance of Jupiter against the peasants of Libya, who refused her water, and the peasants, already metamorphosed, some half, and others entirely, into frogs and tortoises, are placed on the edge of the different tablets, and throw forth water upon Latona in every direction, thus forming liquid arches of the most beautiful effect." Walking down the green velvet lawn, we came to the Bassin d'Apollon. Apollo, the God of Day, is emerging from the water in a chariot drawn by four horses, and surrounded by a throng of sea-monsters. Several other fountains represent the seasons. Spring is represented by Flora and Summer by Ceres. Winter appears in a group representing Saturn surrounded by children; and Bacchus, reclining upon grapes and surrounded by infant satyrs, represents Autumn. Near the Tapis Vert, in the midst of a dense grove, is a magnificent rotunda composed of 32 marble columns, united by arches and supporting a number of marble vases. Under the arcades, are a circular range of fountains, "and in the middle is a fine group of the Rape of Proserpine."

The largest and most splendid fountain in the park, is the Bassin de Neptune. Upon its southern border stand 22 ornamental vases, each with a jet in the center. Against the same side, are three colossal groups in lead. The central one represents Neptune and Amphitrite seated in an immense shell and surrounded by tritons, nymphs and sea-monsters. On the left is Oceanus resting upon a sea-unicorn, and on the right, Proteus, the son of Oceanus. There are several other groups; and from the jets of these, amounting to some 55 or 60 in all, issues a deluge of water, when the gates are opened. A quarter of an hour in advance of the appointed time, about 15,000 persons had assembled upon the circular terrace, facing this magnificent fountain, and were waiting with breathless anxiety to see old Neptune take his turn. We had seen the wonders and beauties presented by the other fountains as they shot their silvery columns, and clouds of vapor high into the air, or spanned their pyramidal basins with innumerable liquid arches intersecting each other in every conceivable direction; but the grandest sight, it was said, was still in store for us. All the other fountains had commenced their playing with humble spasms—the columns rising higher by degrees, but old Neptune took every body by surprise. Hundreds leaped and shouted for joy, when they saw that the southern heavens, which had been so clear and beautiful but a moment before, were suddenly whitened with clouds of vapor upon which the rays of the western sun produced a most charming effect. A gentle breeze gave to each spouting jet, a misty tail, comet-like in appearance to the admiring spectators.

AN INCIDENT

which added much to my pleasures and enjoyments of that glorious day, deserves notice here, as it illustrates that if one even starts to make the tour of the world alone, so that he may not be deained by the loiterings of a companion whose astes and fancies differ from his, need not therefore be without pleasant associates when he is in vant of them. Early in the afternoon, as I was bout taking my seat under the shade of a yewree on a terrace where I might have a fair view of Bassin de Latone, (the play of whose liquid arches ender it the most *beautiful* of all in the garden), I was accidentally met by the same English party with whom I had traveled from London to Paris. It was a happy meeting indeed, and the incidents of our walks and conversations upon that pleasure-garden will ever remain fresh and green on memory's tablet. They had finished their tour of Germany and returned in time to spent the great day of the month at Versailles. As the band was discoursing excellent music, the fountains playing, and crowds of people streaming hither and thither in the midst of these splendid scenes, one of the ladies passed a remark which I only learned to appreciate fully, several months afterwards. She said, "*I love the quiet English Sabbath.*" Her father had experienced before what the continental Sabbath was, but his daughters, though they appreciated these charming scenes none the less, would have preferred them on week-days; for, nearly a month of sight-seeing among a people who keep no Sundays such as we do, had made them long for a day of sweet and silent repose. Several months later, after I had traveled through France, Belgium, Germany, Switzerland and Italy, withou finding a day of rest such as England and Americ make of their Sundays, I felt that even the pleasure seeker should rest one day in seven. Often thought of the "quiet English" and America Sabbaths.

CHAPTER X.

LEAVING PARIS.

On the 6th of August, after a stay of fifteen happy ays in Paris, I began to make preparations to ›ave for Brussels. I had walked during that time ccording to my daily register, about 140 miles, ıaking an average of over 9 miles per day, for I ould not avail myself of the omnibuses and city ars, as I had done in London; because I could .ot make myself understood in French.

Paris had presented so much that was new or adically different from what I had seen elsewhere n the world, even London not excepted, that I felt ustified in addressing the following conclusion to ,n American journalist:— In Paris, there is such , harmonious combination of civilizing and refin-ng instrumentalities and influences, which, if I do ıot elsewhere find a nearer approach to than I ıave thus far, will not only throw sufficient light ıpon the question, " How does she lead the nations n thought and fashion," that the most thoughtless nay be able to solve it, but which will even entitle ıer to be styled *queen of cities and Capital of the so-›ial world.*

As I had definitely decided to return from Fgypt ;o America by way of Paris, in order that I might ›ee the great city once more toward the end of my tour, and be the better qualified to estimate he true position in the world, I made a little bundl of the guide books and views, which I had alread accumulated on my trip, and also dropped som of the superfluities of my wardrobe—these thing I gave into the care of my chamberlain, and bad good-by to Paris for a season. My friend and tuto Prof. P. S., accompanied me to the station an bought me a ticket for Brussels, as we call it in ou language, but the French and Belgians call i Bruixelle (pron. Broo-ĭx-el). My friend informe me of this and gave me a drill on pronouncing th word correctly, for if I should have called it Brus sels, no Frenchman would have understood wha I meant. I was now about to leave the only ac quaintance that could speak my language, and g to another people of the same strange language a the Parisians speak, with no right to expect that I should be so lucky again in meeting a suitabl companion. I had ordered my mail to be for warded to Cologne, Germany, until September 1st At 11:15 p. m., August 6th, the train moved away with me toward Belgium.

I had forgotten to ask how often and where I must "change cars" from Paris to Brussels, and now, where no one understood either English or German, what could be done! Possibly, I need not make a change all night; and perhaps I should at the next station already! How readily my friend could have informed me, had I only asked ıim! But I managed to keep the right track, hough at the expense of considerable anxiety and he sacrifice of some rest and sleep that I might ›therwise have enjoyed during that night-journey. ˙ learned a lesson, however, which aided me in ıvoiding such perplexities in the future. As soon ıs we reached the first station, I ran to a conduc- ›or and, holding up my ticket, cried out, "Broo- .x-el?" He understood me and motioned me to keep my seat. Some accommodating Frenchman soon told me that he was traveling the same way for a considerable distance, (as his ticket also made clear to me), and offered kindly to inform me when I had to leave that train. My peace of mind being thus restored again, I made a pillow of my satchel and went to sleep.

The next forenoon (Saturday, August 7th) we reached Douane, where we had to pass muster under the Belgian custom-house officers. I was now with the wooden-shoed Belgians. A large company of the poor peasants passed muster with me. Each was provided with a pick or a hoe, or both, lying over his shoulder, and a large flaxen bag of other implements, &c., suspended from it. Nearly all wore caps, and the whole company looked very shabby, indeed. My clothes were in strange contrast with their tattered garments, for there was not another well-dressed passenger in the whole company; and I felt like one out of his element, because I did not also have a pick or hoe! A hundred Belgians with a hundred bundles crowded into several small apartments of the station, found little room for their careers, which consisted of the irony ends of their picks and hoes, so that those occasionally hooked the prominent points of the faces of those immediately behind them! Strange to say, these collisions did not provoke any to insults or the use of vulgar adverbs, but gentle reproofs kept them all cool and steady till we entered the cars again. The reader will pardon me for saying that a similar crowd of persons in this country, placed under the same tempting and exasperating circumstances, would have created a row in five minutes, as would be the natural consequence if there were but a single ruffian in the whole lot. Nothing will strike the American tourist more when he comes to the Old World, than the good order which prevails everywhere. To meet two persons scolding and insulting each other, is an extremely rare occurrence. The orderly behavior of such a company of peasants will impress one more with the importance of teaching the young, lessons of patience, humility and *obedience* (which latter quality of character is the mother of a hundred virtues), than volumes of dry philosophy on social ethics will generally avail.

I saw an elderly lady kiss a middle-aged man alternately upon each cheek; an incident that is common in European social life, and that shows how the affections of the heart are cultivated and find expression. In Brussels I saw a son rest his hand affectionately upon his mother's shoulder, as they stood amongst the multitude in a public square.

I reached Bruixelle (Brussels) at about three o'clock in the afternoon. In order to see what kind of money was in circulation in Belgium, I immediately bought some pears of a fruit-woman, and handed her half a franc (10 cents). You may imagine how I was perplexed when the lady handed me a dozen coins of various sizes and values, as my change. Knowing, however, that though the coins had different impressions, the system was the same as that of French money, I murmered to myself, "Blessed be the Decimal System," and went to some retired quarter to count it! One piece was a large whitish coin marked 10c., and worth 2 cents in our money; others were centimes, which are equivalent to but one fifth of our cent! I soon learned to know them all.

After having taken a long walk through the city, I engaged a room at a hotel where one of the boarders could speak a little English, and soon retired to take an afternoon nap. I awoke to broad daylight, but did not at once know whether it was *that day*, or *the next day already;* and there was no one about, just then, whom I could have asked! As the sun was standing in the western sky, I concluded that it was more likely that I had slept only a few hours, than that I should have slept 27 hours; and when the landlord was contended with the payment of one night's lodging, I felt satisfied that I could not have stayed two nights with him! On Saturday afternoon, after my nap, I went out again to see the city. Brussels is one of the most progressive capitals in all Europe. Several splendid boulevards lined with fine cafes and large edifices adorned with innumerable balconies, reminded me of Paris and its architectural scenery. It has a passage that compares well, both in brilliancy and magnificence, with some of the grandest in Paris. The Bourse de Commerce, (just completed), with its four elegant facades, would do credit to any city, and its market houses are among the finest that I have ever seen.

On Sunday (August 8th) I found all kinds of business being transacted, just as is done in Paris. On my way to the Cathedral, I met a dozen dog-teams that Sunday morning. Quite a small dog will draw a larger cart load of milk, than I would have expected that half a dozen of them could pull. The milk is distributed over the city by women, principally. It seems strange, how much work must be done by the women, where the men are required to spend a large portion of their time in the service of their respective countries, constitutting the large standing armies with which Europe is flooded. Some of these women have large dogs to draw their milk-carts, others have smaller ones hitched to one side and assist them by pulling themselves on the other side of the shaft!

THE CATHEDRAL (ST. GUDULE),

is a grand old church, some portions of it dating from the 13th and 14th centuries. "It is rich in old stained glass and monuments. The carved wooden pulpit by Verbrüggen (1699) represents the expulsion of Adam and Eve from Paradise." The choir renders excellent music. An odd feature in the religious exercises of this church, is the manner in which the choir is noticed when to sing, by the ringing of a common bell.

HOTEL DE VILLE.

Hotel de Ville (the Town Hall) is an elegant building dating from the 15th century. It is four stories high to the roof, besides there are 4 rows of dormer-windows in the roof (four stories in the garret!) Its graceful tower is 506 (?) steps, 364 feet high. The view from the top is magnificent. Behind this building, at the crossing of two fine streets, stands the curious "mannikin ——" statue and fountain, evidently a relic of the *shameless age.*

I spent some of my time with an intelligent merchant who had been traveling in America, and could, in consequence, speak the English quite well. He informed me that he was not aware that Belgium had any Sunday-laws upon her statutes. Any one may do upon the Sabbath-day everything that he might do on week-days, if he feels so inclined. On Sunday afternoon, I left Brussels for Antwerp (Anvers). Nothing can be more delightful than the rural scenery of Belgium. The whole country is as carefully tilled as a garden—every foot of available soil being under cultivation. Most of the dwelling houses are small, but everything about the houses, yards and gardens is kept in the most perfect order. Occasionally, a beautiful vista opens to a fine residence in the distance. As we rode along in the cars, we would occasionally see an afternoon or evening party seated around a richly laden table glittering with glassware, and enjoy their dinners and suppers under some shade trees in the midst of their gardens. This custom is common in Europe, and presents most beautiful and homely sights.

Soon after I had entered the cars, I noticed that the tone of the conversation among the passengers was different from what I had been accustomed to hear in France and Belgium thus far. I now heard the chatter of the Dutch, but understood no more than if it had been so much French. Dutch and German are two entirely different languages. Dutch print in the newspapers does, however, not look so perfectly strange, as the conversation sounds to the ear.

After arriving at Antwerp I was soon found by a porter who conducted me to a German Hotel. How social and hospitable these Germans are—and, I must add, Europeans in general. *Die "Deutsche Wirthschaft"* (German Hotel) occupied quite a small building, which presented a very ordinary appearance on the outside, but I shall never forget that carpeted bar-room, the costly furniture of the parlor, and the accommodating landlady which we found there. Taste and comfort are always consulted, even where the greatest simplicity prevails.

ANTWERP

is one of the most Catholic cities (some say the most Catholic city) in the world. Its streets are filled with images of the Virgin and Child, the Savior and the Cross. These stand at the corners of the crossings, or preside over the street lamps. On one of its church towers, over a gas light, is represented a candle stick with the rays emanating from its light. On each side, is a little cherub—one has a cross and the other an anchor. Over them, stand the mystical letters "IHS," the cross being combined with the H after the fashion of a monogram. Beneath is the following inscription:

GELOOFD
ZY JESUS CHRISTUS
IN HET ALLERHEYLIGSTE
SACRAMENT.

In another part of the city I found a representation of the crucifixion, the cross upon which Christ is nailed being about 20 feet high. Effigies of two women in oriental costume stand on either side of it.

In Antwerp, as in Brussels, the spirit of progress has seized the leading circles, and the hand of improvement has commenced tearing down her ancient houses and building new streets upon the modern plan and style of architecture. One of the most handsome avenues in the world, being from 290 to 350 feet in width, and about two miles long, runs through the very heart of this city. It has several moderate angles, which render it convenient to assign different names to different sections of it. Avenue du Commerce reaches from the northern end of the city to its magnificent squares in the center, known as Place de la Commune and Place de la Victoire. Here begins Avenue des Arts, which, with Avenue de l'Industrie, leads to the southern confines of the city. These avenues consist of three parallel roadways with two broad foot-pavements between them, and wide pavements at the sides. Let us cross this avenue from one side to the other, and estimate the width of its different parts. First we cross a broad pavement of perhaps 30 feet; then a roadway of about 50 feet; next a foot-pavement lined by thick rows of trees whose branches form an arch over it; then the central roadway, perhaps 150 feet wide; and afterwards, another foot-pavement, a roadway and the pavement on the other side, corresponding with those already mentioned. The great square in the center of the city occupies about 6 acres. In this section of Antwerp, nearly all the old buildings have been torn down and new ones erected during the last few years; and in many other sections the same work of widening streets and erecting new buildings in place of the old, is being done with reckless haste. It seems as if old houses were regarded as a disgrace to the city. That few images are to be seen in the new sections of the city, is a sure sign that commerce, art and industry (see the names of three avenues which run through this city) have sounded the tocsin of revolution, and that the ancient religion with its emblems, forms and ceremonies, is yielding to the spirit of modern civilization and refinement, as many other cities of Europe have already done.

It is aremarkable fact, that as Catholicism sinks in Continental Europe, its communicants will not stop to join Prodestantism, but go strait over to Rationalism. France, for example, has had these two extreme elements fighting each other for the ascendency, for a long time, and no middle-road sentiment ever gained a foothold. Prodestant Europe will cling to the church the longest, and, do we not already see the indications very planely that after all Europe has turned rationalistic, America will continue to cherish the church and built her a Rome for future generations to bless as the fostering mother of modern Christianity?

NOTRE DAME CATHEDRAL.

The Cathedral is the most elegant Gothic Church in Belgium, and one of the most famous in the world. Some parts of it date from the 13th and others from the 16th centuries. The spire (403 feet in height) is a proud rival of that on the Cathedral of Strasbourg, and its chimes of 99 bells are deservedly famous. Within the church, are some of the most celebrated paintings of Rubens. Among them are "Descent from the Cross," (considered his master piece), "Elevation of the Cross," "Assumption" and "Resurrection." The interior of this church is ornamented with master paintings and fine works of art in lavish profusion. The cathedral is free in the morning, but at noon the paintings of Rubens are unveiled, and a fee of 1 fr. is charged for admission. There were about 35 other tourists there during the afternoon that I visited it.

The Church of St. Jaques contains the tomb of Rubens, and many pictures, a number of them veiled and shown only for a fee.

THE MUSEUM.

The museum contains some of the best (most natural) paintings in Europe. The pencil of Rubens has imitated nature so perfectly that the eye almost fails to detect a flaw in the execution. The spectator may know that he only stands before a flat surface of paper daubed with paint; but his soul will be stirred, his pulse begins to beat faster and his imagination runs away with him, as he looks at such masterly executions of a skillful hand as is the "Dead Jesus" and some others in this museum. The congealed blood in his side, upon his hands and on his head, with the tears of

Joseph and Mary and others, so natural that one mistakes the pictures for the reality, create feelings in the beholder such as he seldom experiences elsewhere, even in Europe. He first mourns for the dead and pities the afflicted; then he recovers himself again, and thanks the artist for having given him a key to the thoughts and feelings which he himself must have cherished while executing this painting. It is said, that when Roubiliac was erecting the Nightingale monument in Westminster Abbey, described on page 86, "he was found one day by Gayfere, the Abbey mason, standing with his arms folded, and his looks fixed on one of the knightly figures which support the canopy over the statue of Sir Francis Vere; as Gayfere approached, the enthusiastic Frenchman laid his hand on his arm, pointed to the figure, and said in a whisper, 'Hush! hush! he vil speak presently.'" Can we conceive that Rubens painted the "Dead Jesus" without sobs and tears?

I had seen acres of paintings in the Kensington Museum in London, in the Louvre in Paris and in Palais de Versailles; but it was reserved for me to see the paintings of Rubens and of Van Dyck last, so that I might know their merit.

Near the entrance of the Museum, stands a fine monument and statue to the honor and memory of

ANTONIO VAN DYCK
P.
CIↃ.IↃCCC.LVI.

No one would wish to leave Antwerp without having seen the "gilded halls" by the river side, containing some of the most brilliant apartments in existence.

Antwerp has a population of about 120,000 inhabitants, and is the chief sea-port of Belgium. The Scaut Fleuve (River Scheldt) is from a quarter to a third of a mile wide at Antwerp.

CHAPTER XI.

HOLLAND.

Early on Tuesday morning (August 10th) I tarted on "a run through Holland."

The Meuse and the Rhine form numerous nouths, and their deltas are low and marshy. A nost magnificent bridge crosses these, which is everal (three?) miles in length. Fourteen immense ron arches are required to span one of the mouths of he Rhine. Much of the land is lower than the ocean, and a great conflict is waged between the Hollanders and the Sea, for the possession of the and. It is a strange sight to see vessels sail along he embankments higher than the chimney tops of the houses along the shore! Watchmen are stationed along these embankments and when the ocean breaks a leak, they will ring the alarm bells and every body will arm himself with a spade or shovel and run to the sea-shore to battle with the water. Thus have these people defended their property against the encroachments of the sea for many centuries.

A great part of Holland is as level as the ocean, and there are neither fences nor hedges to be seen. But ditches surround every little field and lot, and innumerable wind-mills pump the water that gathers into these ditches, up into canals, which intersect the country like a net-work, and conduc the water to the sea. Extensive meadows and ricl pasture land support large herds of fine cattle an(sheep, which constitute the wealth of Flemish in dustry.

These Hollanders have some very curious style: of dress, and, like the Swiss, still wear their ancien costumes, even after the rest of Europe have adoptec the fashions of Paris. In the larger towns anc cities, however, the tide of revolution has set in and the young belles and beaux have commenced to "sail in Paris styles." A few years more, and the traditional costumes of the Flanders will have disappeared altogether.

The men are very partial to "burnsides" and wear their hair pretty long, combed wet and stroked down so as to look smooth and glossy. The old women, in place of ear-rings, wear ornaments in the form of immense spirals suspended from the ends of half of a brass hoop that passes around their heads below their white caps. These hang down over the cheeks and are almost as long as their faces. Some of the young ladies coming in from the rural districts, carry a head rigging—I do not know what else to call it, for it is neither bonnet, hat, nor cap, nor any combination of these; but it is an apparatus for the head that baffles description, and which, for want of a better name, we must call a *tremendous thing*, both in magnitude and in design! I have seen women with straw hats hat must have been well nigh a yard in diameter! n The Hague, I saw little girls, however, (from 6 ɔ 12 or 15 years of age) that were dressed as tidily nd looked as fair and as sweet as any of our ımerican school-girls.

PUBLIC HIGHWAYS.

In Holland, these are *highways* in fact as well as n name. They run in perfectly strait lines through he country, are about a yard higher than the neadows at their sides, and are lined by thick ows of willow-trees. They are turnpiked of course, s are all the roads in civilized Europe. From hese roads the traveler has always the same field of vision—a circle around him that is about 8 to .5 miles in diameter. Towering spires may be een in all directions. I visited Dordrecht, Rotter-lam, The Hague, Amsterdam, Utrecht, Arnheim and intermediate places.

THE HAGUE,

n Dutch 'S Gravenhage or 'S Hage, in French La Haye, is the capital of Holland as well as one of ts finest towns. "It was originally a hunting seat of the Counts of Holland (whence its name, 'S Graven Hage, 'the Count's enclosure')."—*Hurd and Houghton's Satchel Guide to Europe.*

The supreme attraction, is the museum rich in the best paintings of the Dutch school. "Here is Paul Potter's world renowned 'Bull,' alone worth a trip to Holland to see." This famous picture represents a rural scene. A ram, a ewe, a lamb, a bull and a cow are gathered together under an ol tree, and the old farmer, standing somehow be hind the tree, taking a look at them. It is so pe fectly true to nature that one can hardly persuad himself that the living animals are not before hin The pictures known as Rembrandt's "School c Anatomy" are also as deservedly famous. Wha ever the criticism of one who is no artist may b worth, it is my opinion that Rubens's paintings an some of those in this museum, are the truest t nature of all that I have seen in Europe. Raphael' paintings in Rome are shady in comparison t those of the Dutch school.

Tuesday, August 10th, 4:21 p. m. Leave Th Hague for Amsterdam, where I arrived at 7:30 p m., having passed Haarlem at 6:45 p. m. At 8 o'clock, as I sat on the platform of the Oosterspoor weg Station, the bells of three different towers commenced simultaneously to chime their peals and that too with mathematical precision. The exactness with which the clocks in the clock-towers of Europe keep time is remarkable; and the music of the pealing bells is beautiful, when numbers of them chime at the same time.

At Amsterdam I was asked for my passport, I told the "blue coats" that I had it in my satchel. "You should have it with you," said the German-speaking official. I replied that I had not been aware of that; and as I had not been asked for it either in England, France or Belgium, I had placed it into my satchel, so as not to wear it out in my pockets. I sent the porter to fetch my satchel, took the passport from it, and, after having shown it to the officials, placed it into my pocket again, so that I might have it ready in any emergency. These officers were very accommodating to me afterwards, however, during the time that I waited for the next train for Utrecht. After having had quite a social chat with them, I asked them what they would have done with me if I could not have produced them a passport from the government of my country. "Well," said one of them, "we would have been obliged to subject you to an examination, and if your answers would have satisfied the committee, you would have been allowed to pass on."

CLOAK-ROOMS.

In connection with the railway stations, wherever I traveled in Europe, there are "cloak-rooms," in which the baggage of the travelers is stored away. It costs 1 to 2 cents to have a package, parcel, umbrella or satchel deposited into one of these, and then the depositor receives a receipt or check for his luggage, which he must present when he wishes to have it again. But Holland offers none of these excellent accommodations, else I would have spent a day more among these Flanders. When I came to Amsterdam, I was immediately assailed by a herd of porters, each anxious to take my satchel into charge. It had been my rule to carry it to the cloak-room myself, but here I could not find one! After a vehement struggle with the fierce porters, one of them who could say "Yes," in German, and who nodded his head when I asked him whether he would take it to a cloak-room, took it and carried it into the station, a distance of about fifty feet. But they kept no cloak-room as I observed when it was not placed into a special apartment for the purpose. It did not seem home-like at all to me, so I asked the agent whether he would give me a receipt for it. "Yes, if you satisfy the porter, I will," he answered. This reply made me more tired of Amsterdam than anything else, for, thought I, if the agent of the would-be "cloak-room" is a party to such a set of fellows, I must indeed have fallen into pretty bad company. I offered the porter 4 cents, which was twice as much as it cost me in other cities to have my satchel cared for a whole day, but he refused to take it. Being unwilling to become the victim of their extortions, I took my satchel and carried it (almost three fourths of a mile) through town to the Oosterspoorweg on the other side of the city. There I obtained good accommodations. I had asked for lodging while coming through the city, but could not suit myself; so I decided to start that evening with the first train for Utrecht. How different was the social atmosphere of the Oosterspoorweg Station! Not only were the porters and the officers civil, but there was an excellent restaurant connected with it, and the waiting-girls of the coffee-room were tidily dressed in French costume, spoke German, and were social, polite and accommodating.

At 9:30, I left by train for Utrecht, which I reached at 10:35 p. m. The station was a new and spacious one and the accommodations were again like those which I had been accustomed to, before I saw Holland; so I felt quite at home again.

UTRECHT.

It is entirely wrong for the tourist to come into a strange city late at night, but I could not avoid it this time on account of my sudden determination in Amsterdam not to spend the night there, as had been my intention. A clever and kind-hearted gentleman accompanied me through comparatively dark streets, and found a good hotel for me.

The next forenoon I ascended the high tower (469 steps, 321 feet in height). In this tower, at the height of 124 steps, lives the lady custodian of this stupendous building. She must have "*high* times" up there! The tower is a large square structure affording plenty of room even for several families; but I was thinking that she must have quite a time of it carrying up her water and all the numerous other things necessary to house-keeping.

The view from the top of the tower takes in the greater part of Holland. The country all around is quite level, as far as the eye can see. Level, in

Holland, *means* level. Here one sees the innumerable wind-mills, and the labyrinthic net-work of canals which intersect Holland. An almost boundless expanse of meadow land stretches out in every direction, and affords excellent pasture to the lowing herds that roam upon it. One sees but a few scattered trees, and several small woods, all the rest is clear and bear—no hedge-fences even to interrupt the dull monotony of the scene below. A strong wind, and it was high too, whistled around that lofty tower, reminding me of our winter storms when they whistle over the chimney-tops—a music that often makes melancholy hearts home-sick.

It was exactly 12:00 o'clock, and I was in the middle of the sentence, "How beautiful these bells chime," when a boy motioned me to come quickly to a certain place where I could see the cylinder revolve which communicates with the peal of bells.

Two points of lightning-rods crown this tower. Few lightning-rods are to be seen upon private buildings, in Europe, but upon public buildings they are occasionally met with.

I must not leave Holland without once more referring to the rattling of the wooden shoes upon the pavements, the red artificial flowers which old gray-headed women wear upon their heads and the gaudy colors of some of their dresses; also to the universal custom of carrying everything upon their heads.

The denominations of Dutch money are *florins*

or *guldins*, and cents; 100 cents equal one florin. The florin is equal to 40 cents in United States money.

At 12:38 p. m., I left by train for Cologne, Germany. By 1:00 o'clock we entered a desolate section of country consisting of barren sandy soil, scanty crops, and dwarfish shrubs and trees. On our way, I formed the acquaintance of an elderly gentleman who moved from Holland to this country nineteen years ago. This gentleman explained to me the agricultural institutions of Holland. He now lives in new Holland, Ottowa Co., Michigan, a town of 3,000 inhabitants, most of which are natives of Holland. There are about 15,000 more of his native countrymen living in the neighborhood of new Holland and at Grand Rapids. They have a newspaper published in their language in this country. At 2:25 we reached Arnheim where my Dutch friend left me.

At Zeevenaar (near the boundary between Holland and Germany) we passed muster. Soon after we crossed the Rhine on a ferry, which carried us and the whole trains of cars over together. Thence we rode through Rhenish Prussia on, on, until we reached Cologne.

CHAPTER XII.

COLOGNE.

Köln, (or Cologne), the principal town in the Rhenish Province of Prussia, the seat of the supreme court of justice for the west bank of the Rhine, one of the chief commercial cities in Germany, and a military stronghold of the first class, is an old Catholic city dating its foundation from the 1st century of the Christian era. In the beginning of the present century, it had 200 churches and chapels; it has at present 25 only, two of which are prodestant.

THE CATHEDRAL.

The first place that the traveler naturally goes to visit is the Cathedral, (Ger. Dom), which "is perhaps" says Bædeker, "the most magnificent Gothic edifice in the world." This superb edifice is over an acre and a half in extent! It is 448 feet long and 249 feet through the transepts; the choir is 149 feet high. The magnificent south portal cost more than $500,000.

The central portal in the west end is 93 feet high, and 31 feet wide. The central window is 48 feet in height and 20 feet wide. The projected height of the twin towers is 511 feet. These are intended to consist of four stories, the third of which is approaching completion. A model representing in miniature what this structure is intended to be in the height of its glory when its towers are completed and crowned with spires, may be seen in a store adjacent to the *Dom-platz*, where the "only veritable" Cologne water (eau de Cologne) may also be obtained.

The foundation of this vast edifice was laid in 1248. Little work was done at it between 1322 and the beginning of the 16th century, and none from the latter date until 1816, when its restoration was begun under the auspices of the King of Prussia. Since that time $2,000,000 have been expended upon it. Those lower portions of the walls which were built 600 years ago, are old and gray and washed thinner by the rains of those half a dozen centuries. Such as appreciate the poetry of architecture, see in its multitude of spires and finials (large and small) a thousand vegetable forms, uniting to produce a bewildering effect upon the imagination; but no word-picture can do justice to the almost matchless beauty of this fine blossom of Gothic architecture. The tourist will love to go round about it and inspect and contemplate its every part, to take near views and distant views of it, and to revisit it time and again; and when he has bid adieu to Cologne and returned to his far distant home, he will dream dreams, by day and by night, in which he revisits and beholds again the beauties and glories of this magnificent temple.

St. Ursula, a church that is said to have been

been built in the 11th century, contains a monument erected (1658) to St. Ursula, a princess of England, who, according to the legend, when on her return from a pilgrimage to Rome, was barbarously murdered by the Huns at Cologne with her 11,000 virgin attendants. The skulls and bones of these martyrs are preserved in cases placed round the church. Large sections of the walls in the church are shelved and divided into pigeon holes, each containing a skull! I saw no less than 600 or 700 of these skulls (by actual count). The bones "are worked into the walls in a species of sepulchral mosaic." These bones, it is said, had been in their graves about 400 years. The old pictures of the apostles are painted upon slates, one of them bearing the date 1224.

In the Golden Chamber are preserved the most sacred relics; here is a bone which is claimed to have been in the right arm of St. Ursula, while a gilded shrine contains the rest of her bones. Do these identifications not prove conclusively that anatomy was better understood when these bones were classified than it is even now? The name of the anatomist who selected St. Ursula's bones from among 11,000 and identified them is not given, but he certainly deserves much credit for it. Here are thorns from the crown and a piece of the rod with which Christ was scorged, one of the six jars of alabaster used at the marriage in Galilee, and a piece, about as thick as a hair and an inch or two long, of the "true cross." So they *say*. These things were brought hither from Syria by the crusaders in 1378.

THE MUSEUM.

The Museum in Cologne is one of the most interesting that I have yet seen. Its curious old paintings carry one back to the wretched times of the middle ages, when nothing but superstition and the night-mare of hell could influence predatory man to humanity on civil order. A picture of the Last Judgement is characteristic of the religious notions of those early times. In this, Christ is represented as sitting on one rainbow and resting his feet upon another. To his right stands a beautiful castle, into which numbers of beautiful persons are going. But on the left, how horrible! A massive time-worn citadel from whose large chimney tower issue flames and smoke, into which winged devils are descending, while others, carrying wretched-looking men in their clutches, fly about near it, or are approaching it with their struggling victims, and hideous monsters of quaint, fantastic forms accompany them in their excursions! One of these hideous beasts is represented with an extra head upon one shoulder and one under its breast; it has also faces upon its knees!

Among the other relics of antiquity, is Cheopetra with a little snake creeping over her bosom. Christ on the Cross surrounded by Mary and the Apostles, Madonna in an arbor of roses, Lions Fighting,

Mourning Jews, Summer Night on the Rhine, and Galileo in Prison, deserve special notice among the hundreds of other admirable paintings.

A fine iron bridge 1,359 feet long, and wide enough for a double line of rails and a separate roadway, crosses the Rhine directly east of the Cathedral.

In traveling through foreign lands, one sees so much that is indecent, obscene, and shockingly profane, according to his our way of thinking, that he scarcely knows what to include and what to suppress in his accounts of foreign manners, customs and institutions. Some writers incline to the policy of rendering a true account of what they touch, but will restrain their pens from giving any notice of about one fourth of all they see, because they do not wish to pain the feelings of their readers by reciting to them narrations of horrible tragedies that occurred in the past, or of groveling superstitions that prevailed; such as we all wish had never disgraced the history of infant humanity or constituted the day-dreams of our ancestors. They carefully select that which flatters and pleases the vanity of their fellows, and pass by unnoticed, everything else. This course may tickle vain people, but it cannot meet with favor among those who love the truth, and the whole truth. There are sins of *omission* as well as of *commission*, and writers betray and deceive the world as much by the former class as by the latter. Some fastidious writers are afraid to call things by their proper names, considering it more appropriate to paint an African with a brownish color than to shock the beholder with a picture of a man with a *black* face! I can not take the reader through Europe in that way. To paint a negro we need *black* paint, and to describe scenes which are unfamiliar we need words and language that is not used in the drawing room or parlor every time we meet. So much for the introduction to an episode that is characteristic of the profanity of some of the descendents of the old Teutonic stock, when they become exasperated. The second day that I spent in Cologne, I went to a German barber to be put into trim for making my descend into the lower latitudes and consequently warmer countries. Another customer was ahead of me. While the barber was at work upon him, all the time in a rage and swearing *barber*ously at some proceedings, a thunder storm came up very suddenly, and so obscured the light of the sun (though it was midday) that he could not see to go on with his work. Hereupon he began first to swear at the clouds, then at the Lord himself, using all the epithets of abuse that he could find in his entire vocabulary of profanity, there were heavy peals of thunder and vivid flashes of lightning, but, the darker it became and the more tremendous the crashes of the thunderbolts, the more the senseless and exasperated barber cursed and swore. After the shower and hail, I walked out into the pure fresh air and under the blue vault of heaven smiling down upon the refreshed vegetation, and tried to draw a picture of that profane man's mental panorama, but I never succeeded even to this day. Such behavior is not of rare occurrence, else I should not have related it; but even sacred history refers to similar incidents. The wicked, it is recorded, danced and were merry even until the waters of the flood swept them away.

A certain divine related to me a similar story concerning the behavior of a large body of the passengers with him on the "Great Eastern," when she was foundered at sea and obliged to return, after they had advanced 500 miles. When the storm was assailing the great ship, breaking down its masts and tearing away its rigging, so that most of the passengers were in despair and expected to sink any hour, they kept prayer-meetings almost continually. Another faction found fault with these, declared that praying was an intolerable nuisance and asked the Captain to prohibit it. The Captain decided that he would not interfere, whereupon the party offended took to dancing, cursing and swearing, and tried their utmost in this way to break up the prayer-meetings.

I heard similar profanity on my return trip across the Atlantic. One night when a storm assailed our ship, so that the waves rolled over the deck and the fierce rocking of the vessel threw many almost out of their beds, I heard many of them swear, even during the very time that the thunder rolled with tremendous roarings and crashes across the heavens. It seems almost impossible that conscious intelligent beings could behave thus, but the fact that they do, helps us to believe other strange truths recorded in history, without which, no correct conception of man's former depraved condition can be formed at this advanced day. For example, few seem to appreciate the part played by the Catholic Church with her images, shrines, sacred relics, and magnificent temples, in taming and civilizing man, because they do not know who and what he was when the light of intelligence first began to direct his footsteps, and he had not yet learned to control his selfish nature which had hitherto been guided by an instinct worth a hundred times more than intelligence without morality or religion. We make a sad mistake yet in the nineteenth century, in cultivating the intellect and leaving morality so much out of the question. We see some of the fruits already in the corruption which prevails alike in all circles without regard to party or sect. I will recur to this again in speaking of the influence of the church, when I come to describe the magnificent churches of Italy.

On the second afternoon that I spent at Cologne there had been a shower, and from sunset till dusk I beheld one of the grandest atmospheric phenomena that I had ever witnessed. From a window of Mlüler's Hotel (facing the *Dom-Platz*) I was looking over the Cathedral at the western sky, as the sun throw its colored light through the small drops of rain still descending, and thus colored both the green foliage of the trees and the grand edifice before me, presenting a scene of such enchanting beauty as would afford almost a sufficient excuse for one to go into raptures, or sink down in a fit of ecstatic delight.

I may add that before leaving Cologne, I saw among the many dog-teams used in distributing produce over the city, a span whose disproportion I shall never forget; there was a dog hitched to one side of the shaft and a woman took hold of the other side and assisted him in pulling the load!

BONN.

On Friday morning, August 13th, I left Cologne and went by rail to Bonn, 21 miles further up the Rhine. It is the seat of the Freidrich Wilhelm University, and contains about 26,000 inhabitants. The Poppelsdorfer Allee, an excellent quadruple avenue of fine horse-chestnuts, three quarters of a mile long, is the principal promenade of the town. At the end of it stands the Schloss containing the University, with a library (200,000 volumes) and a museum rich in Roman antiquities. The Münster (or Cathedral) dates from the 12th and 13th centuries. In the Münsterplatz stands a fine bronze statue of Beethoven, a celebrated German musician, who was born in the Bonngasse, No. 515. This statue faces south, (as do most of the statues that I have seen in Europe, except when the surroundings are unfavorable). One side of the pedestal contains the following inscription:

LUDWIG
VAN
BEETHOVEN
GEB. ZU BONN MDCCLXX.

The other three sides contain base reliefs representing muses playing upon musical instruments.

Half a mile above the Poppelsdorfer Schloss rises the Kreuzberg (400 feet high) crowned with a white church. This contains the "Holy Steps," 28 in number, which must only be ascended on the knees, and are in imitation of the Scala Sancta at the Lateran in Rome, piously believed to be the identical steps of the Praetorium ascended by the Savior when he appeared before Pilate.

The view from the tower of this church is one of the most beautiful on the Rhine. After enjoying the scenery a while, with a party of ladies and gentlemen whose society I had joined in the church below, we came down, and I took a rustic seat on an eminence and surveyed the beauties of the landscape more at leisure. The most beautiful part of the Rhine is from Bonn to Mayence, and this view from the Kreuzberg constituted for me a fine initiation into the charming scenery that fell to my portion to enjoy the coming three days. Large sections of the country here are entirely without fences, there being no hedge-fences even, and the landscape checkered by the different fresh colors of the various crops, spreads out like a beautiful carpet of green, red, yellow, gray, and a dozen other tints and shakes, all mixed up, or like a pavement rich in mosaics. We had also gone into the cellar of the church to see the skeletons and bodies of 26 *Servitten* lying about in boxes or coffins set in rows upon the ground. These, it is said, built the church in 1627. The bodies of several of them seem to have petrified more or less perfectly, but the rest of them are mere skeletons, and present an anatomical display that reminded me of what I had seen in St. Ursula, in Cologne, as above described. This cellar is perfectly dark and is entered by a trap-door in the form of a heavy stone, which an attendant removes by means of a crowbar. The steps leading down are narrow and the passage very low, so that several of the ladies at first declined to enter, but we persuaded them, however, to accompany us. A tallow candle afforded us some little light, and after brushing away the cobwebs which the spiders had spun since the last party had made their entry, we came upon the sickening sight of the dozen or more skeletons still preserved. The ladies in the party were intelligent and dressed tastefully, and I shall never forget how the gaudy colors of their dresses contrasted with the gloom of that nasty cellar.

The frequent odd adventures into such places as many would not like to enter in their own homes in the presence of their friends and companions, constitutes a prolific source of amusement. After we had crept out of that dirty cobwebbed passage, our clothes were slightly soiled and cobwebby. With the remark, "If we were all with our fashionable circles at home, I suppose we should not go on this way," or some such allusion, that reminds the company of how differently they are wont to go on at home, one can, under such circumstances generally provoke a fit of merriment. To the traveler, every day is a day of adventures—frequently of rather funny adventures!

At 2:30 p. m., I left Bonn by rail for Mehlen, (5 miles further up), where I crossed the Rhine on a ferry and came to Königswinter on its right bank. Southeast of this village lie "The Seven Mountains" (Siebengebirge). From the Drachenfels (1,066 feet high) the view is the most picturesque, and this one, about a mile from the village, I ascended. Donkeys and donkey boys are found here in aboundance, but I would have nothing to do with the donkey, and immediately set out to make the ascent on foot. I did not come far before a girl crowned me with a wreath made of leaves, and asked me to buy it. The scenery is so romantic, here, that many will yield to the importunities of these poor girls and give them a *groschen* (2½ cents) and make the rest of their journeys with wreaths of leaves upon their hats! The ruins of the castle of Drachenfels (or dragon's rock) erected in the beginning of the 12th century, is near the summit of the peak. The cavern of the dragon may be seen from the Rhine half way up the hill. "This dragon was slain by Sigfried, the hero from the Low Countries, who, having bathed himself in its blood, became invulnerable."

The summit of Drachenfels commands one of the noblest prospects of the Rhine. Here sat Byron when he wrote the following beautiful lines:

"The castled crag of Drachenfels
  Frowns o'er the wide and winding Rhine,
Whose breast of waters broadly swells
  Between the banks which hear the vine;
And hills all rich with blossomed trees,
  And fields which promise corn and wine
And scattered cities crowning these,
  Whose far white walls along them shine,
Have strew'd a scene which I should see
  With double joy went *thou* with me."

While luxuriating here amidst these grand and beautiful scenes of the Rhine, we were visited by a shower, after which I enjoyed the sublime sight of *looking down upon a rainbow* which stood in the valley below me!

That evening I rode by rail to Ehrenbreitstein which is opposite to Coblentz.

CHAPTER XIII.

COBLENTZ.

On Saturday afternoon, August 14th, I prepared a programme of my contemplated trip through South Germany, Switzerland, Italy and the East, which, together with several hundred cards, I got printed in the afternoon. By means of these programmes I informed my correspondents in America, in which cities I would look for mail matter and at what times I expected to reach them.

Mr. Ellner, of the *Coblentzer Volkszeitung,* told me that the dialects of the German language are so different, that the people of Coblentz and those of Cologne can scarcely understand each other when they speak their peculiar dialects.

The principle, that whenever a stream of water makes a curve, the outside bank (that which turns the water from its strait course) is always more precipitous than the other in proportion to the amount of curvature of the stream, is well illustrated at the confluence of the Mosel and the Rhine at Coblentz, by the course of the latter. The waters of the Mosel flow almost perpendicularly against the right bank of the Rhine, and have helped it in forming the precipitous rock of Ehrenbreitstein rising to the height of 387 feet above the river, upon which stand the famous fortifications of that name.

The Rhine curves toward the left for about six or eight miles, and its right bank is in consequence high and steep, while the left bank is in the form of a gradual slope, bearing a striking resemblance to the valley of the Jordan for a mile around Siegersville, Lehigh Co., Pa. Another principle, that the width of a valley and the hardness of its bed is always in proportion to the fall of the stream of water flowing through it, does also find as ample illustrations in the sweeping Rhine as in any of the humbler streams whose courses I had watched and studied at home. These two principles afford perhaps the strongest and most conclusive of all proofs, that the hills and valleys of our planet are all the result of erosion.

The streets of Coblentz are mostly narrow, as are also its pavements, many of the latter being only from one to two feet wide. There are several remarkable churches, one, the Church of St. Castor dating from 1208, being an example of the early "Lombard style."

In order to enjoy the Rhine scenery to the greatest advantage, I took passage on a steamer to Bingen, and started out on Sunday morning at 10 o'clock. One of the steamers had been delayed about three hours that morning on account of the fog, but the day turned out to be a most beautiful one. I took a seat near the prow of the steamer, where I could conveniently watch the views of both banks without interruption from any source. I was now about to ascend the most romantic part of the Rhine —the Rhine of history and of poetry, upon whose precipitous banks the Germans erected their castles in the early and middle ages and defended their "Fatherland" against the attacks of their warlike neighbors. Only after one has seen the castled steam with its numerous watch-towers crowning every towering peak, and the indescribable beauties of this noble river, will the national air, "Die Wacht Am Rhein," (Watch At The Rhine), seem so beautiful to him, as it does to the sons of Germany, whose souls are stirred by its boundless historic associations.

I cannot stop to describe the scores of Schlösser, (castles), the charming prospects, the beautiful valleys with their verdant hill-sides peeping into the Rhine, and the rich vineyards upon its sloping banks in some places, or the romantic scenery of the bare rocky mountains that rise almost perpendicularly at its sides to the height of 300 to 500 feet, in other places. Several objects claim particular attention, however.

Some 35 or 40 miles up the river from Coblentz, on the left bank, rise the imposing rocks of the Lurlei to the height of 433 feet above the Rhine. The river is very narrow in this place, has much fall and makes a decided turn, so that it is with considerable difficulty and some danger that steamers make their ascent. The river is here 76 feet deep and its waters form a whirlpool, (Gewirre).

This place and every other one of interest along the Rhine, as well as all its castles, have their legends. It is said that a siren who had her abode on the rock, was wont by means of charming music to entice sailors and fishermen to their destruction in the rapids at the foot of the precipice.

As it is dangerous for steamers to meet on these rapids, they have a rule that every steamer coming up the stream must fire a few small cannons as soon as it approaches the Lurlei, so that steamers that are descending may hear it and wait to let the ascending steamer pass before they enter upon the rapids.

Near Bingen is the Mouse Tower, so called because the cruel Archbishop Hatto, of Mayence, had once compared some poor famishing people to mice bent on devouring corn, and caused them to be burned in his barn after having invited them to come there and receive provisions which it had been his duty to give them. After this outrage he was immediately attacked by mice, which tormented him day and night. He sought refuge in this tower, but was followed by his persecutors and soon devoured alive. Thus runs the legend.

We reached Bingen at 3:30 p. m., and started by rail for Frankfort on the Main an hour later. At 7:15 we crossed the Rhine by the magnificent iron bridge at Mayence, from which we had a good view of the extensive fortifications of that city, also the rich decorations of the entire city with banners, for, though it was Sunday, the Republicans (Internationals or Communists as they call themselves) had a great political meeting. I formed the acquaintance of one of their number who traveled with me to Frankfort and gave me an invitation to accompany him to one of their meetings the next evening. The Communists which fled from Paris after the storm of 1871, are now busy in different countries assisting those opposed to royalty to form organizations for the purpose of instituting other revolutionary movements some future day.

FRANKFORT.

Frankfort, the home of the Rothschilds, down to 1866 a free city of the German Confederation and the seat of the Diet, has a population of 90,000 inhabitants. It has 20,000 Catholics and 8,000 Jews.

The Römer is historically the most interesting building in Frankfort. It became the town-hall in 1405. In the second story is the Kaisersaal (Imperial Hall) containing the portraits of 47 emperors reigning from A. D. 912 to 1806. In front of it is the Römerberg, (a large square), or market-place, which was the scene of public rejoicings on the occasion of the election of an emperor. After dining in the Kaisersaal he would show himself from the balcony to the assembled multitudes upon it. Down to the end of the last century no Jew was permitted to enter it.

The Judengasse (or Jew's street) was founded in

1462 and until the beginning of the present century all the Jews of the city lived there in an isolated community. Every evening and on Sundays and holidays, this street was closed with gates, and a Jew who would venture into any part of the town was subject to a heavy penalty.

The Church of St. Paul is immediately behind the Römer. It is a circular building having seating capacity for 3,000 adults, and was used in 1848–9 for the meetings of the "German National Assembly for remodeling the Constitution."

Frankfort is the birthplace of Goethe, and has embellished one of its squares with a fine monument to his memory. It has also a fine monument to Schiller and a magnificent one to Gutenberg.

In some of the old streets of this city the upper stories of the houses are built out over the streets, making a break in the wall at every story, so that some of the narrow streets are thus almost arched over.

I left Frankfort by rail on the 17th of August, at 2:00 o'clock, and reached Darmstadt at 2:40 p. m.

Before leaving home, I had been presented by different persons with the addresses of a number of their friends and acquaintances in different countries of Europe, and also with letters of introduction to them. On account of my unbounded success in forming congenial friendships with foreigners, I never departed from my programme in order to meet persons for whom I carried letters, and consequently met none of them except a young American lady who had been abroad for several years with the object of studying the German language, and who was now connected with an educational institution at Darmstadt. Though I had been almost continually surrounded by tourists whose society and friendship I enjoyed and appreciated, still this meeting with a friend of one of my friends at home, seemed to me just like meeting an old acquaintance. We seated ourselves under a tree in the beautiful garden belonging to the Boarding School, and had a long talk about what each had seen in Europe, and how the social, political and literary institution of the Old World differ from those of America. The next day my new friend kindly accompanied me through the large museum contained in the Schloss, comprising a valuable collection of about 700 paintings, among them some fine specimens of the Dutch school. The Library in the Schloss consists of 450,000 volumes. On our way to the Schloss Garden we saw a little hut nestled in the garrets of other large buildings and surrounded by them on every side, except one of its gable-ends. The old peasant (so says tradition) would not part with it for any price, therefore his neighbors built their houses *around, beneath* and *over* his, leaving but *one* side clear through which he could admit the light of heaven into his humble apartment! Darmstadt has about

40,000 inhabitants, and is one of the cleanest and most modern in appearance of all the cities that I met in the Old World. Its broad and shaded streets intersecting each other at right angles, give it much of the appearance of an American city. The view from the Ludwigsäule commands a fine prospect of the level country around, with its large woods of "tall trees" so rare in Europe, and the Rhein Strasse (Rhine Street) loosing itself only in the distance, is the straitest and longest street that I have yet seen.

WORMS.

Worms is one of the oldest towns in Germany. "The war against the Saxons was planned here in 772, and here the great contest concerning the investure of the bishops with ring and staff was adjusted by the Concordat between the Emp. Henry V. and Pope Calixtus II." It had once 70,000 inhabitants, but it contains now only 15,000, (⅔ Prodestant).

The *Cathedral* is a remarkably fine Romanesque edifice with four elegant towers, and two domes. The towers are adorned with odd figures of animals and gurgoyles. Most of this church dates from the 12th century. In the pediment is "the figure of a woman with a mural crown, mounted on an animal, whose four heads (angel, lion, ox, eagle,) are symbols of the four Evangelists, the whole being emblematic of the victorious church."

"In the Bishofshof was held the diet of April

1521, in which Luther defended his doctrines in the presence of Charles V., six electors, and a numerous assembly, concluding with the words: 'Here I stand, I cannot act otherwise, God help me! Amen.'"

The Baptistry contains some curious sculptures. Upon the roof of the building (stable) represented in connection with the Nativity, there lies a wheel, the signification of which no one could tell me. Among other musical instruments represented in relief in this church, there are the harp, the bugle and rows of violins or fiddles!

In the Luther-Platz stands the great Luther Monument, an imposing memorial of the Great Reformer. Its execution occupied nine years and cost $85,000.

CHAPTER XIV.

DIE PFALZ (PALATINATE).

From Worms I went to Frankenthal, where I spent the night (of August 18th) at the Pfalzhof. It was now nearly two months since I had left America, and since that time, in all my wanderings, I had met no people that resembled the Americans. Even in Germany had I not yet seen any one whose physiognomy spoke of near kinship to any that I knew on the other side of the Atlantic. But at

FRANKENTHAL

I was introduced to a new class of experiences which were as unexpected as they were pleasant. If I had not here experienced it, I could never have anticipated the feelings of a lonely wanderer who, when thousands of miles away from home, was addressed in tones so like unto the voices of those he loved to hear at home, that he felt as if he was all the time hearing familiar voices in every direction.

At Worms my attention had already been arrested by social phases that reminded me of America, but at Frankenthal I met an officer at the station, who, upon being asked where the peculiar Palatinate dialect was spoken, not only mentioned to me the places, but also gave me a list of fälzish words that are peculiar to them, most of hich are purely Pennsylvania German both in heir pronunciation and their meanings. A young irl at the hotel and her brother not only used lanuage similar to ours, but betrayed their kinship n various other ways. I spent about a week in Iannheim, Neustadt, Speyer and the surrounding ountry, during which time I devoted all my atention to the question of our common ancestry. That those people are cousins to many of our ennsylvania Germans can easily be proved in a ariety of ways, even when we throw aside the traitional and historic evidences which we have that nany Pennsylvanians have emigrated from the Pfalz in times past. The most convincing proof o those who can not go there and see the people hemselves, likely consists in the fact that many of he family names of the Pfälzer and of our Pennsylvania Germans are the same. I attended the large annual Sängerfest at Neustadt, in which 973 singers from all parts of the Pfalz participated. I procured a catalogue of their names and found that a very large proportion are the same as those of the majority of our people. When we contrast with this the fact that the proportion of names common between our people and that of any other section, is much smaller, we see the force of the argument. But this is by no means the first thing that strikes the visitor. Consanguinity or relationship by blood betrays itself in a hundred ways. Particular words and expressions, peculiar pitches o the voice, styles of address, forms of salutation and special ways of performing certain kinds o work, tell their tale with an emphasis that makes itself understood even to the unscientific observer The expression of the face and the very ring of the laugh often impressed me with the truth that it was that of a cousin's brother or sister. I often expressed my surprise at these things to those around me, and by a free indulgence in the peculiarities of their idiom enlisted the attention and gained the friendship of those people with magical effect. From Frankenthal I went to

MANNHEIM,

which is the most regularly built town in Germany. It is divided into 100 squares like a chess-board, and has about 40,000 inhabitants. It consists of 20 sections lettered from A to U (the J being excluded from the nomenclature) and the squares of each sections numbered from 1 to 5. As the city enlarges in territory the numbers of the squares run from 5 upwards. The streets are named as in other cities, but the houses are numbered *around* the squares. Thus the *Mannheimer Familienblatter* (a newspaper published in the Pfälzisch dialect, which is like the Pennsylvania German) is printed at E 1. 8.—Section E, Square 1, No. 8.

NEUSTADT.

At Neustadt I made my home for half a week

whence I took excursions into the country. One day I went to Drachenfels, walking about 16 miles in the woods, where I had nothing but paths and guide-boards to lead me; but the latter are found wherever two paths meet, so that I could easily find my way back again. In order to meet these people in every sphere of life, I used to go out to see the poor men and women work in the fields. One Saturday afternoon I struck out from Landau toward the Haardt Mountains with a view to put up for the night in a certain town that I saw on a distant hill. When I had come a short distance, I overtook a little maiden whom I asked the name of that town, so that I might ask the way thither if I should come into a valley where I could not have pointed it out any longer. I pleased the young girl very much by presenting her with my card, and induced her to use her glib tongue volubly in telling me about their schools—what they studied, how long the terms last, &c. She would get along very well in our Pennsylvania German dialect. When we parted, she skipped away and proudly showed the card which she had received from an "American," to one of her schoolmates (?). Here one may see women hauling hay and grain with cows, though I also saw some men use horses. Toward evening I met a peasant of Böchingen, who had finished his work and was about to return home. On learning that I was an American, he asked me to accompany him to his village, saying that *Kirmes* had come, the grea jubilee season of the year when all the churche were being re-dedicated, after which ceremony th people would go to the public houses and keep u dancing and drinking wine and beer from Sunda noon till Monday night, and that I could therefor see a great many Palatinates together in his town I asked him what hotel accommodations their tow had; to which he replied that there were severa hotels and he would conduct me to a good one On reaching the place I accompanied him first tc his home and was introduced to his family. I hac here one of those opportunities, so rare to th traveler, of seeing the kitchen arrangements of th middle and lower classes. When we came to the hotel he asked the landlord for a room for me, whc immediately came to me and explained that on account of the great "Fest" (anniversary) he had turned all the spare rooms of the house into coffee-rooms, "but," said he, "though I know that Americans are used to good accommodations, I can only offer you the *Fruchtkammer* (granery) to-night, where I have a good nice bed for you, however, if that will suit you." The homelike cheerful tone and conversation of the landlord at once captivated me, and when I looked at the large house and saw all his rooms already filled with guests enjoying their wine and beer together, after the German fashion, I soon decided to stay with them. The room which he gave me was a very large one in the second story of the house, and, though there were large heaps of grain and different kinds of farming implements there, the end where the bed stood was clean and inviting, considering the circumstances. There was no lock at the door, but the landlord's honest face and assurances soon put me at ease about that matter. He told me that I might place some barrels against it, however, if I felt so inclined, which of course I did. There was a lady in that town who had been spending her time in Philadelphia for several years, but who had on this occasion come home to Böchingen on a visit. An invitation was sent to her in the evening already, asking her to come to the hotel where an American was waiting to meet her, and early on Sunday morning she met me in the coffee-room where we spent the morning. One's partiality to the English language seldom displeased me in Europe, but as this lady was a native of that part of the Pfalz whose people spoke a dialect more like the Pennsylvania German than I heard anywhere else, I insisted upon conversing with her in "the dialect." The landlord who did not understand any English was with us most of the time, so that out of respect for him she also felt constrained to speak German when he was present, but whenever he left us she would speak English, the language of her new American home. She had visited Allentown, Pa., and was well acquainted with the resemblance of the Pfälzish and the Pennsylvania

German dialects. I went home to Neustadt that forenoon and attended the great Pfälzer Sängerfest (the annual Concert of the Palatinate Choirs). The city was splendidly decorated with flags, and the "Fest" was a grand success in every respect. From Neustadt I went to Speyer, and a day later to

HEIDELBERG.

Heidelberg was the only place where I found lady ticket agents at the railway station. The station is a very large and important one, and the positions held by those ladies are of great responsibility. In Continental Europe, it is the ladies that transact most of the business in almost every city. Hotels, stores, shops, cafes, drinking stands, &c., are generally managed by ladies.

Heidelberg was the last city in which I felt that I was hourly seeing the cousins of the Pennsylvania Germans. Here still, I did occasionally see one who not only favored some of our people in form and features, but whose voice and accent also spoke of kinship. I had heard persons speak in some parts of the Pfalz and particularly around Böchingen (about 10 miles S. S. W. from Neustadt and 25 miles W. S. W. from Speyer) from 50 to 70 per cent. of whose words corresponded to the Pennsylvania German. Dürkheim, Landau, (and some say, Kaiserslautern too), are good examples.

The old renowned university of Heidelberg has 800 students, and a library of 200,000 volumes and 1,800 MSS.

The castle is the most magnificent ruin in Germany. The towers, turrets, buttresses, balconies, and fine statues still stand there, proud and bold, even in its ruins. And the portcullis of iron in one of its lofty gateways gave me the first idea how the balance of the enemy could be shut off, after a portion had been admitted into the yard of the fortifications with a view of slaughtering them. The iron bars of this portcullis or sliding gate are very thick and heavy, and have sharp points below. A tower stands over the gate, into which the portcullis is drawn up. The defenders of castles would sometimes conceal themselves and keep perfectly silent on the approach of an enemy, as if the castle had been abandoned, but as soon as as large a portion of them as they thought they could dispose of, had entered, the portcullis was dropped, which, on account of its immense weight, of course made its way to the ground even if it had to pierce the bodies of a dozen that stood under it! Hereupon the alarm was sounded and all that were inside were barbarously slaughtered. In some castles there were large pit-falls full of pointed spears standing upwards. As soon as a large part of the enemy were upon this pit, they would be precipitated into the spears below! At other places there were immense rollers, and only one approach to the castle, which lead directly up the hill. When the assaulting enemy made its approach by this, and the hillside was filled with the enemy's soldiers, these rollers would be loosened upon them, and thus the bodies of many thousands would be mangled in a minute! Such was the barbarity of the ancients.

I will not forget the long walk I had all alone through one of the underground passages of the Heidelberg Castle. I saw a pale light at the other end, when I entered; but it was dark in the middle, and turned out to be much longer than I had anticipated. These passages are about 7 feet high and 10 feet wide, and are arched by a brick vault. The illumination of this ruined castle on the evening of August 23rd, constituted one of my grandest sights in all Europe. It seemed to be enveloped with flames of such an intense heat, that its walls, towers, &c., appeared to be about to melt down! As the colors of the illuminating light changed suddenly from yellowish white to blue, green and red, the scene was so indescribably beautiful, that numbers of the ten thousand spectators actually went into raptures.

THE TUN,

in the castle of Heidelberg, the largest of all the tuns in the world, is 32 feet long, 22 feet in diameter at both ends and 23 feet in the center. Its eighteen wooden hoops are 8 inches thick and 15 inches broad, and its 127 staves are 9¾ inches thick. The bung-hole is 3 to 4 inches in diameter. To built it cost the enormous sum of $32,000, and its capacity is equal to about 2,200 common barrels! On top of it is a dancing-floor having the bung-hole in the center! What a joy it must be for the dancers to reflect that there is such a flood of wine still beneath them! This giant tun erected as an altar to the jovial God "Bacchus," has been filled completely three times, (1753, 1760, 1766).

"In Heidelberg beim grossen Fass
Da liess sich's fröhlich sein,
Bei einem vollgefülten Glas
Von edlem Pfälzer Wein;
Den als dies Fass kam einst zum stand
Do war ein Jubel in dem Land,
Da freut' sich Alles, Gross und Klein,
Denn voll war es mit Pfälzer Wein."

"In Heidelberg, the 'Grosse Fass,'
Caused merry days to shine,
When all enjoyed the well filled glass
Of noble Pfälzer wine;
For when this Tun first came to light,
All did in joy combine,
To see the 'Fass,' oh wondrous sight!
Fill'd up with Pfälzer wine."

The Philosophenweg, (Philosopher's way), two miles in length, commands some of the finest prospect on the Rhine. It winds through charming vineyards, and from it may be enjoyed splendid views of the town, castle, valley, and of the beautiful outlines of the Haardt Mountains and the cathedral of Speyer in the distance.

From Heidelberg I went to Stuttgart, remarkable for the vast collection of books (300,000 vols.) in the Royal Library. Among these are about 9,000 Bibles, in some 80 languages!

The Railway Station in Stuttgart is remarkable both for magnificence and the beauty of its interior. Its wide and lofty passages and splendid waiting-rooms, are among the grandest in the world.

From Stuttgart I went to Carlsruhe, famous for the manner in which the streets meet at the Castle, from every point of the compass. Some thirty streets meet here like so many sticks of a circular fan. Near the Botanic Garden, is a large Hall of Art rich in paintings and relics.

STRASSBURG.

Strassburg, the capital of Alsace and Lorraine, is situated on the River Ill, 2 miles from the Rhine, and comprises a population of 80,000 inhabitants. Its Cathedral, covering more than an acre of ground and 216 feet in height, is deservedly famous. Its elegant spire, the highest in Europe, is 465 feet in height. To procure a permit from the city authorities to ascend to the "lantern," which is immediately below the extreme summit, I walked about the city nearly an hour to find the proper official. The view from the platform or roof of the building (216 feet high) affords a fine view of the beautiful plains of Alsace, but many ascend to the "lantern" simply for the satisfaction of saying that they have done it. No one is allowed to go higher than the platform, except by special permission from the city authorities, and accompanied by a guide and protector, for which an extra ticket is required. The ascent is quite easy for some distance, but by and by the spire becomes too narrow to have stairs on the inside, so that we had to climb up on the outside along ladder-like steps. If one would become giddy in this place, he might fall from a hight of over four hundred feet into the street below! I cannot stop to speak of the world-renowned astronomical clock which is contained in this cathedral.

The railroad through the Black Forest is one of the great victories of civil engineering which characterize this age of great undertakings. We passed in exactly one hour through 38 tunnels, during which time, in our ascent of the mountains, we passed through one valley three times! When we had reached the highest point, we saw the two other tracks at different elevations on the mountain side below us! Here we passed for many hours through pine forests, all the trees of which were raised from seed, (some sown and others planted). Many square miles of this mountainous section is covered with pines planted as regularly as our orchards; and the scenery of these mountain-sides green with dense forests in which the comical tree-tops stand with mathematical exactness in the square or quincunx order, is among the most beautiful imaginable.

CHAPTER XV.

SWITZERLAND.

It is almost impossible to describe the scenery of the Alps to one who had never yet ascended mountains above the region of the clouds, without so bewildering his imagination that his fancy will call forth and accept more fictitious notions than true ones. The best description that I had ever heard of the Alps, was the occasion of my most incorrect conceptions about them. I think the speaker did not misstate or exaggerate anything in a single word, but as he could in an hour's talk tell only one tenth of what one ought to know, in order to form a correct notion of what the Alps look like, my fanciful imagination promptly supplied the coloring of the other nine tenths of the picture which he left untouched; and consequently when I came to see the Alps, I found them entirely different from what I had anticipated.

The ordinary school maps represent the Alps as extending along the borders of Switzerland, as if they consisted of a single range, or possibly of several parallel ranges, and Mount Blanc as its towering peak. With what surprise a scholar who only saw these maps, will look about him, when he reaches the summit of any high peak in Switzerland! On the Rigi, for example, one sees an extent of territory almost 300 miles in circuit, every part of which is studded with ice-capped peaks. These range not in any one particular direction, nor do they number only several dozen, but many hundreds of them stand around the beholder toward every point of the compass and at variable distances, from the Pilatus near by to the most distant part of the horizon—more than 50 miles away. The snow-clad crowns of many of these rise high above the clouds, so that

"Through the parting clouds only
The earth can be seen,
Far down 'neath the vapour
The meadows of green."

Those forms of clouds called cumuli, (P. G. Gewitter Wolken), presenting themselves the appearance of mountains covered with ice, often creep around these peaks at less than half their height!

At Zurich I first beheld the strange sight of mountains and clouds piled upon each other so that I could not well distinguish them. It was on a sunny afternoon that I stood on the banks of the *Zuricher See* (Lake Zurich) and, looking over its calm waters, I beheld in the distant southeast a strange phenomenon. There stood the high glittering banks of clouds, and over them I saw the black sides of a towering peak whose top was covered with ice and snow. I then visited the Rigi and looked at Alpine Switzerland from its giddy heights. This, since the railroad has been completed to its top, is one of the most famous mountains in Switzerland. Though it stands beneath the line of perpectual snow, its top being covered with grass in summer, still it commands a panoramic view of indescribable grandeur. Numerous hotels stand around the top where thousands of tourists find shelter during the summer nights, and among them is one of the finest hotels in the world. When fall comes, all the landlords must take their families and move down from the mountain, as it would be impossible to keep the track of the railroad clear during the winter to bring up the necessary provisions for them. The snow is often from 10 to 20 feet deep on these Alps.

All Swiss scenery, whether one is on the lakes, upon the mountains, or in the valleys and ravines, is singularly charming, and bears no resemblance to the scenery which one sees elsewhere; so that for this lack of having something with which to compare it, no one can do it justice in any description short of a volume. The reader will therefore pardon our haste in this country. One who sees the rest of Europe and not Switzerland, will not miss any particular links in the historic chain of social, religious and political development of the human race, but he will not have seen the sublime in nature. The Alps are the poetry of inorganic creation, and a week or two spent on their lakes, in their valleys and gorges, amid the high waterfalls or upon their snowfields and glaciers, teaches one to associate new meanings to the words, grand, sublime, lofty, inspiring, overawing, romantic, wild, precipitous and bewildering, &c. It took me two days to ascend as high as the Rhone glacier, during which time I walked over 30 miles up hill along old military roads which the Romans constructed through Switzerland. I saw the snow and ice on the first day already, and it seemed as if I was but a little below it, but in place of reaching the snow line in the afternoon as I judged I might, I did not reach it until the next afternoon at 5:00 o'clock. The valleys are narrow and the mountains rise in some places almost perpendicularly at the sides, so that the snow and ice which melts near the tops of the mountains, falls down thousands of feet into the streams below. Water-falls that are from several hundred to a thousand feet in height are numerous among the Alps.

The Giessbach Falls which I ascended on the 6th of September, descends in a series of seven cascades 1,148 feet, and the Handeck Falls, which I passed on the 5th, precipitates in an unbroken sheet from the height of 250 feet! Rainbows stand over all the falls of the Alps, whenever the sun shines.

On the second day (Sept. 4th) of my ascend of the Alps, I could look upwards and see the eternal snows, or look down into the valleys, and see the people in the meadows and fields making hay or cutting grain! Haymakers may drink the water that was an hour before part of the mass of ice and snow which they see hanging near the top of the mountains several thousand feet above their heads! Avalanches slide down into the valleys every month of the year, and I passed through tunnels and bridges that are purposely constructed that the snow may thus slide over the roads without doing harm to any one. Where the mountains rise too precipitously, it is in some places impossible to construct a road along the edge; in these cases they pierce through the mountains for considerable distances. The Axenstrasse, along Lake Luzerne, has many such tunnels, one of which is about one eighth of a mile in length. In the Grimsel, the road avoids a water-fall by passing through a tunnel under it.

The Rhone Glacier, the only ice-field that I crossed, is upwards of nine miles in length and rises from 5,751 feet to 10,450 feet in height. About the time of sunset on the 4th of September, I entered the cavern of ice from which issues the stream that constitutes the source of the Rhone River. "This is the Rhodanus of the ancients, which was said to issue 'from the gates of eternal night at the foot of the pillar of the sun.'"

I descended through the Grimsel pass (7,103 feet) and Haslithal along the upper waters of the Aare down to Meiringen, in one day. Though there is only a bridle-path through the almost unparalled wildnesses of this valley, still there is a telegraphic wire running up to the hotel at the upper end, near the Rhone Glacier! No language can describe the picturesqueness of the bare rocky sides of this valley. I heard persons who thought they were alone, utter a dozen exclamations of surprise while making a single turn where a new view opened! The solitary tourist will ejaculate his exclamations without number; and it is under such circumstances that the unpoetical soul seeks some personification to whom it may do homage. It would not require a worshipper of images to kneel down, in the Grimsel or Ober Haslithal, before any emblem that embodied any adequate representation of the crushingly sublime scenery that one beholds there!

I met a lake whose depths seemed as boundless as the blue heavens above me. The water of many of the Swiss lakes is as clear as crystal, so that white objects at their bottoms may be discerned at great depths.

While sailing along the Lake of Geneva one day, I could as little see substance in the water below me, when I looked upon it at a certain distance from the steamer, as in the clear sky; both seemed alike blue and boundless!

The weather and the temperature changes very suddenly among the high Alps. The climate in the valleys of Switzerland is as warm as ours, in summer, while some thousand feet higher lie the everlasting glaciers. From these, avalanches of cold air precipitate into the valleys, so that the mercury often falls from 20 to 30 degrees in ten minutes! One is in danger of taking "a cold" every day in Switzerland.

Besides "The Alps" and the *lovely lakes* among them, the tourist may also see castles, museums, art galleries, pleasure gardens, &c., in Switzerland, but I will only enumerate a few of the most striking objects that I met and saw in this curious country, and then pass on to Italy.

One of the bridges of Lucerne is adorned with very curious paintings representing the "Dance of Death." Scores of skeletons, some blowing the bugle or playing with the triangles, others equipped with hoes and spades, are jubilant over their work!

One of the finest organs in Europe is the far-famed one at Freiburg, having 67 stops and 7,800 pipes, some of them 33 feet long. This instrument has such a range of volume that it can simulate the roaring thunder as well as the faintest echo. The portal of the same cathedral which contains the famous organ is also adorned (?) with a curious representation of the last judgment. St. Peter leads the blessed to the door of Heaven, but half a dozen evil ones busy themselves in disposing of the wicked. One of them that has a head like a hog, carries them from the scales into a large caldron where they are boiled. Others with forks in their hands pitch them into the mouth of the large dragon-devil who is represented as glutting them, and whose capacious mouth admits of several of them at a time! The time has almost arrived when one may no longer describe what he sees in the churches of Europe! This reminds me of a monster that stands upon a fountain in Bern, called the Kindlifresser, (the Ogre), who is in the act of eating a child, while others doomed to the same fate protrude from his girdle and pockets!

Berne is a great place for bears. Besides those connected with the curious machinery of the clock on one of its clock-towers, among the dead bears, they also keep a large den of living bears at the expense of the government. The bear is the heraldic emblem of Switzerland, as is our eagle of American freedom.

Of the fictitous hero, William Tell, and the nature and character of the Swiss Republic, I can not say more in the compass of this book, than that the former is a myth and that the latter was in a great measure the outgrowth of poverty.

The reader may form an idea of the miserable dwellings of the peasantry on the mountains, when he is told that many are hardly distinguishable from the stables in which the cattle are sheltered.

When I came into view of Guttannen, the first village of any considerable extent that I passed after seeing the Rhone Glacier and the wildnesses of the Grimsel and Haslithal, where no houses except hotels, and in some places not even trees or grass abound, I felt glad once more to see a group of human habitations, and determined to count them, so that I might record their number. I passed along the edge of the mountains where I could easily overlook the village, but it was in many instances impossible to determine by a survey of their external appearances, which were the stables and which the houses or huts, so I counted them all, large and small, and found their number between 60 and 90. I once intended to count these buildings only with windows, as houses; but I soon discovered that some huts had windows only on one or several sides, and looked like stables on the other sides!

A question to dairy men: Do thunder and lightning affect fresh milk? A lady keeping a cafe in Brienz, told me that if a thunder storm overtook those which were bringing the fresh milk from the mountains, the milk would suddenly turn sour, so that it could no longer be boiled for drinking it sweet. She said, "*Es thut sie verbolera, so das sie gerinnt wen man sie kochen will!*"

CHAPTER XVI.

GENEVA TO TURIN.

Switzerland has two national languages, the German and the French, both of which are recognized by the Government. Geneva is French, so I had some trouble in getting my information and procuring a ticket for Italy. I left Geneva at 6:40 a. m., September 10th, and after passing through a number of tunnels, one of which required 5½ minutes of moderate railway speed, we arrived at Bellegarde, on the French border, and passed muster. From 9:00 to 10:00 o'clock we were detained at Culoz, and by noon we saw the snow-covered Alps again. At 3:30 p. m., we arrived at Modane and passed muster for Italy.

MONT CENIS TUNNEL.

We entered the mouth of this great tunnel, over 8 miles in length, at 4:58½ p. m., and were exactly 26 minutes in the very bowels of the earth, where absolute darkness reigns. Temperature in the middle, 59° Fahrenheit.

ITALY.

We now come to a country which contrasts as strangely with the nations of western Europe, as those do with America, or as Alpine Switzerland does with the rest of the world. When I parted at Paris with my New York friend, he bound for

Rome, I for the north, we still had our school-boy ideas of Germany, Switzerland and Italy; and I shall never forget the remark which he then made, and which embodied my notions and anticipations perhaps as well as his own. He said, "I suppose we have now seen the brightest side of the picture, the trouble is that scenes will now become tamer as we advance toward the cradle of humanity." I had been pleasantly disappointed almost every time that I entered a new country, but now, as I was entering Italy, I expected that I would surely not see much to interest me except her rich stores of art and the ancient ruins. But less than a day at Turin convinced me that I had by no means entered a country whose people were behind hand in civilization and refinement; and when on my way from Turin to Milan I saw how much clearer and brighter the blue heavens were, how much sweeter the air smelt than any I had ever breathed before, (not excepting that of Paris, even), and how much fairer the people were than any other that I had yet seen, I felt that I must surely be on the border of that charming paradise which the poets make of Italy, but for which I had never given them due credit.

ITALY'S FAIR SONS AND DAUGHTERS.

I now come to a dry subject, especially for old people; but numbers of my young friends, among them several editors and teachers, requested me very earnestly to take particular notice which country contained the fairest specimens of the human species. Why these literary characters are so deeply interested in this question, I cannot tell, but my duty is plain enough—they want "a true and impartial statement of the facts," which I will endeavor to render them. I observed everywhere that *culture* and *personal beauty* always go together. When I came to a city that had clean and beautiful streets and houses, I invariably found good looking people there; but in the rural districts generally, and in suburbs and wretched towns, beauty and culture are at a lower ebb. I now refer to that form of beauty which is dependent upon personal accomplishments and intellectual endowments and culture—that beauty which beams from an intellectual countenance and sparkles from eyes that glisten with pleasure. That is the kind of beauty that renders 90 per cent. of the individuals in all cultivated society acceptable, and 20 per cent. charming and attractive, but which is wanting to nine tenths of those who cannot, or do not, pay attention to cultivation and refinement. There are a very few persons whose forms and features please and fascinate even without the aid of accomplishments. These may be said to be possessed of *native* beauty, which is met with very seldom in all countries that have a climate unfavorable to health. If I had not gone to Italy, I should not have hesitated to give my preference to the mild climate of Paris, where health and beauty are the natural result of a warm temperature, almost semi-tropical in mildness, and where the highest art assists to make every grace shine. But when I saw how nature dotes upon Italy, I felt as if she was only acting the step-mother to the rest of the world. The loveliest portion of Italy is the valley of the Po. One sees fewer sickly or consumptive people in some parts of England, France and Germany, than in our section of America, but in Turin and Milan every person looks hale, healthy, happy and beautiful, from the tender days of infancy to a ripe old age.

Nothing that I saw in Europe surprised me more than to come so suddenly into the midst of a people whose very countenance bear the bloom of youth, even until the gray locks of age appear.

Old age even knows no wingles here! I know that it seems incredible to any one that has never been in warmer climes, but the word beauty has a new meaning here. The glow which is lambent upon the faces of the sons and daughters of this section of sunny Italy, is something that I never saw elsewhere, and that cannot be described. It is a solemn truth, that nine tenths of all the ladies of Turin and Milan are perfect beauties; and I need not say less for the full round forms of the gentlemen. Only after I had observed that several very fair persons, who happened to pass near me, had gray hair, did I notice that the bloom of youth still glows upon the faces of those who are 35 to 40 years of age! When I first came into this paradise of fairy angels, (for a paradise is the valley of the Po), I mistook this bloom of youth and glow of health and vigor for the lambent flames which flash from the countenances of the intellectual—it seemed to me that I must be surrounded by a halo of literary sages and muses, all gifted alike with every grace and charm that nature can bestow or art improve; but when I observed the youths at work in the fields and the maidens at the garden gates, who turned for a moment from their respective tasks to see our train move along, look as happy, as gay and as beautiful as the belles of the cafes and the beaus of the cities, I concluded that it must be the healthy state of the body that makes every face look rosy and bright in this fair and sunny clime. At Milan I asked some of my companions how far this *paradise of beauties* extended southward in Italy. "To Florence," was the answer. But I did not find that to be quite correct, for though Florence may have more fair people than any northern city, the proportion of beauties to the whole population, which is perhaps ninety per cent. in Turin and Milan, cannot be more than 20 or 30 per cent. in Florence. In order to be able to correct any false impression that I might have imbibed in my first visit to the valley of the Po, I paid particular attention to the same subject on my return from Egypt. At Milan there was then an immense concourse of people assembled from all parts of Europe to see Emperor William of Germany and King Victor Emanuel of Italy parade the streets of that elegant city, with a retinue of over 20,000 soldiers; the consequence was, that the fair people of Milan were lost in the multitude. But on my return to Turin, I found that her beautiful sons and daughters, again presented the same dream-like and enchanting scene of a pleasure-garden full of fair and merry beings possessed of angelic beauty, and enjoying their blessed existance just as I had seen them a month before.

I met travelers that say the same thing of Nature's children in other sunny lands—Spain for example. The truth seems to be, that in warm climates only, will man attain that perfect healthy and beautiful physical development which has constituted the model of the artist and the theme of the poet, in every age. I have heard some pronounce the statue of Venus de Medici, the ideal perfection of female form and beauty. It is probably as near as sculpture can reach it, but who would suppose that a white stone could do justice to the beauty of a pure child of nature? The marble may present a most perfect *form;* but what becomes of the glow of life and flush of beauty upon the maiden's cheek, the ruby lips and the grace and elegance of her movements and winning manners? We may speak of ideal beauty in countries where the physical development of the inhabitants is blasted by the severities of the extreme heat and cold of an inhospitable clime, where the blasts of winter make every form shiver for many months of the year; but the superior beauty of the daughters of Northern Italy, if they were placed side by side with Venus de Medici, would laugh that frigid form to scorn! As compared with these, I thought I had seen no others that could either *talk* or *laugh* or *walk!*

The Italians live upon a very simple diet. When I first saw numbers of them make meals of dry bread and fruit, I supposed poverty impelled them to partake of so scant a diet, but by the time I came back from Egypt, I too had learned to sit down and eat dry bread and grapes together, though I could procure meat as cheap in Italy as elsewhere in Europe. It is not advisable to partake of much meat in any warm country. Any one may form an idea of what kind of a consumer of food cold is, when he reflects how much more flesh we consume in winter than in summer. I did not partake of more than half the amount of food in southern Italy and Egypt that I needed in England, Germany or Switzerland, and there is little room for doubt that many Italians do with one third of the amount of food that we require in the severer climate of the Middle States. I was always reminded of the story of "Cornaro the Italian," related in Wilson's Fourth Reader, whenever I saw them eat their simple meals. It is very singular, too, that they should all look full, healthy and robust; and many of us, on the contrary, lean and sickly. Twelve ounces of solid food and thirteen ounces of drink, seems a very spare supply to an American, but I do not believe that it is accounted very extraordinary in Italy.

MILAN.

The praises of the magnificence and splendor of the Cathedral of Milan are sung all over the world. It is nearly 500 feet long and 250 feet wide through the transepts, covering an area of almost *twó acres and three quarters!* The height of the nave is 150 feet! Its entire walls, and its pinnacles, spire and roof are all constructed of fine marble. The spire is over 350 feet high. The marble slabs constituting the roof are about three inches thick; how enormous the weight of that roof must be! Each of the 135 pinnacles or smaller spires is crowned with a statue, and throngs of others (some 4,500)ornament the outside of this magnificent building. The interior of this edifice is one of the most imposing in the world. As I looked at the rich decorations and delicate traceries of its high ceiling, 150 feet above me, I felt as if no human being could be worthy of enjoying such a magnificent view. But, "unless a language be invented full of lance-headed characters, and Gothic vagaries of arch and finial, flower and fruit, bird and beast," the beauties and glories of the temples of Italy, and her unparalleled galleries of art, can never be described. From Milan I went to Vicenza, where I spent a sleepless night in skirmishes with the mosquitoes! The number and variety of obnoxious insects multiplies fearfully as one approaches the topical regions. Thence I went to

VENICE.

As I was very much disappointed with Venice, I shall not occupy much time in describing this *daughter of the sea.* The railway bridge which leads to this city is about two miles long. I expected that a city whose streets are canals and whose carriages are all boats, would present a very unique appearance, but when I once saw them, they were so exactly what I had anticipated, that I felt disgusted and left the city without doing justice even to the vast collection of paintings in the Ducal Palace, which alone is worth going a great distance to see.

SAN MARCO.

The church of *San Marco* is one of the grandest and most wonderful structures in Italy, and I can only refrain from copying Ruskin's very fine description of it, because his account, though true in every particular, would, to one who has never seen any of the architectural glories of Italy, seem more like the attempt of a poet to depict in glowing language the vagaries of a dream, than like the description of an edifice really in existance.

On the Piazza above the portal of San Marco, stand the celebrated bronze horses "which Constantine carried from Rome to Constantinople, whence Marino Zeno brought them hither in 1205; they were taken to Paris by Napoleon in 1797, but restored by the Allies in 1815."

CHAPTER XVII.

VENICE TO BOLOGNA.

In place of spending several days at Venice, as I now think I should have, I left already in the afternoon at 3:35 o'clock, and reached Bologna that evening. It required between 6 and 7 minutes to cross the bridge, over two miles long, which connects Venice with the land. The water is not deep, and most of this bridge is a mere bank of earth running into the sea. It was on account of my being disgusted at the general unpretending appearance of Venice, that I left her so soon. Among the objects of interest that I saw between Venice and Bologna, was a herd of a hundred deer on a hill-side, and the merry bells of stage-teams jingling like our sleigh-bells, but which may be heard in Italy and Switzerland all the year round. When I observed in my Satchel Guide that Bologna has two *leaning towers*, one of them nearly 300 feet high leaning 4 feet, and the other about half that height and leaning 8 feet, I determined to go and see them. They are massive but plain brick structures, and it is difficult to decide which way the higher one leans. The inclination of the lower one, however, is decided, but presents nothing striking or threatening in its appearance. I felt afraid that the Leaning Tower of Pisa might possibly also fail to present anything that was remarkable or imposing to the beholder when I would come to see it once, just as a thousand and one other objects do which antiquity and poetry have rendered sacred and famous; and I walked away with down-cast countenance and took passage for Firenze (Florence).

FLORENCE.

The Cathedral, (Il Duomo), begun in 1298, is 554 feet long, and 334 feet through the transepts. The nave is 152 feet high; the cupola is 138 feet in diameter or about the same as that of St. Peter's in Rome, for which it also served Michael Angelo as a model.

Close by the cathedral is Giotto's Campanile, 300 feet high, the most beautiful of all the towers that I have seen in Europe. The square blocks of many colored marble with which its four sides are coated, produce a richness of effect that is indescribable. Decorated from top to bottom with all manner of statues and architectural ornamentations, "it is like a toy of ivory, which some ingenious and pious monk might have spent his life-time in adorning with sculptural designs and figures of saints; and when it was finished, seeing it so beautiful, he prayed that it might be miraculously magnified from the size of one foot to that of three hundred." The view of this superb structure in connection with the grand edifice (the Cathedral) to which it belongs, opens so suddenly upon the visitor, that he will never forget what feelings of joy and surprise he experienced on making the last turn around the corner, when these splendid edifices leaped upon him so unexpectedly in all their beauty and magesty.

The church of Santa Croce, whose foundation was laid in 1294, is "the Pantheon of Tuscany." It contains the tomb of Michael Angelo, and magnificent monuments of Dante, of Alfiero, of Macchiavelli, of Galileo and of many others of less fame.

The houses in which were born Michael Angelo, Dante, Amerigo Vespucci, Macchiavelli and Galileo may be found and identified by the memorial tablets which mark them.

Piazza della Signoria is the business as well as the historic center of Florence. Here stands the old capitol of the republic, begun in 1298. It was afterwards the residence of Cosmo I. Near this palace is a magnificent fountain of the time of Cosmo I. I cannot tell positively, now, whether the sculpture and architecture of Florence is so much richer than what I saw elsewhere in Europe, or whether the enchanting beauty of sculpturesque and architectural master-strokes at the Cathedral, the Campanile, St. Croce, and the Fountain and Palace in this magnificent square, may not have thrown me into the condition of one in a dream; but I certainly felt all the time that I spent in Florence like one in another world, where scenes of fascinating beauty were surrounding me on every side, and feelings of ecstatic delight precluding me from any but a dream-like enjoyment of the scenery around. I was without any acquaintance or companion the whole day, which in connection with the fact that I was thousands of miles away from the familiar scenes of home, where every object that I contemplated was new and different from what I was wont to see, could not fail to make me feel like one in a dream. I went along the *Portico degli Uffizi* adorned with throngs of statues of celebrated Tuscans, and into the famous Uffizi Gallery, founded by the Medici, and one of the most precious collections in the world. In the *Tribune*, the inner sanctuary of the great temple of art ("the richest room in all the world, a heart that draws all hearts to it") I saw the Venus de Medici, the Dancing Faun, the Apollino, the Wrestlers, and other masterpieces of ancient sculpture; also, among the paintings, some of the best works of Raphael, Angelo, Titian and others. I must however admit that the out-door scenery of Florence charmed me more than what I saw in its world renowned museum. It seems to me, that Raphael and M. Angelo deserve more praise for the inventive genius which they evinced in translating bible stories and poetical imagery into pictures, than for their mechanical execution. To such as understand anything about paintings, it will seem very absurd, of course, that I should presume to criticise the paintings of these great masters, but they must admit that a hundred of those who roam the world and come to see the works of the masters, are ignorant ot painting and sculpture, as I am, to half a dozen that are able to criticise them from the standpoint of one who is himself an artist. The "hundred" unskilled in the fine arts, have as great a desire to know how they will likely be affected by the sight of those works as the half dozen artists are; permit me to speak to the "hundred !" It is true that the paintings of Raphael and Angelo may have faded, but, whatever they may have been when they were first hung to the wall, they now look pale, shady and inferior in artistic execution to many of those of Rubens and of the masters of the Dutch school in general; that is, if we consider nature as the standard and copying it as the only criterion of a master's talents. But for inventive originality of conception, the Dutch masters are no rivals even, certainly not, of the Italians.

Need I repeat that wherever one finds such a rich store of art as in Florence, there too will he find ladies and gentlemen of beauty, culture and refinement? The same fascinating forms and features which characterize the men and women of Turin and Milan, are also met with here, but they comprise a much smaller proportion of the whole population. It is fair to presume, however, that a large proportion of those which I saw in Florence were natives of distant parts of the globe, which streamed thither, by the thousand, to see that charming city. One can nowhere see more intelligent company than in such a place as Florence; but how the most symmetrical and best looking people of all other countries contrast with Italian beauties, none but those few who ever go thither will ever learn to form the least conception of. It has become my duty, however, to record the fact, that the most favored of all countries when they sail into the society of the fair daughters of sunny Italy cast a shadow about them, as we may fancy any human would when coming into the company of the beautiful angels of a heavenly Paradise. Go reader, if you cannot visit Italy personally, and see what the poets say about these people, and believe every word they can say in favor of their charms.

PISA.

From Florence I went to Pisa with the special object of seeing the famous Leaning Tower (1174–1350). It is circular, having 15 pillars in the wall of the first story and 30 in each of the six succeeding ones. On top of these, is another one (the eighth) much smaller than the rest, and probably built upon it after the tower had reached the amount of inclination which it now has. The entire structure is 187 feet high, and 173 feet 9 inches in circumference (according to my own measurement). The walls are from 5 to 7 feet thick. There is a peal of bells at the top, the heaviest weighing 6 tons. Nothing is more evident than that this tower assumed its leaning position by *accident*. It is probable that this structure, which is the finest in Italy except Giotto's Campanile at Florence, was originally designed to be a very high one, (perhaps 300 feet). It is likely that the foundation did not give way until at the seventh story, and that after it came to a stand-still again, they capped it off abruptly by the odd little story which we now see at the top of it. The inclination amounts to about 13 feet. There is a circular pavement around it about 10 feet wide, which has the same angle of inclination that the tower itself has. It is sunk 3 feet into the ground on one side and 8 feet on the other side. Upon careful examination and measurement I discovered that the diameter of the basin thus formed is to the height of the tower, as the inclination of pavement constituting the floor of the basin is to the amount of inclination of the tower.

Let it be remembered, that this tower is not an independent structure, but that it stands near the east end of the Cathedral, as the elegant campanile at Florence stands near the cathedral of that city.

THE CATHEDRAL.

The Cathedral (1063–1118) is 311 feet long, 106 feet wide, and the nave 109 feet high. The great bronze lamp which gave Galileo the hint of the pendulum, still hangs in its nave.

The Baptistry (1153–1278) stands a little distance from the west end of the Cathedral. It is about 120 feet in diameter and its dome is 180 feet high. Peabody considers it "the most faultlessly and exquisitely beautiful building" he ever saw.

These three most elegant buildings, the Cathedral, the Baptistry and the Campanile or Leaning Tower, are a unite in architectural beauty and design, and for effect in external appearance are scarcely outvied by anything that I have seen of the kind in all Italy. No one will feel sorry for having traveled a hundrsd miles to see the " Leaning Tower," and the traveler will observe with pleasure and satisfaction that its two companions are even more elegant than itself.

On Tuesday noon, September 15th, I left Pisa for Rome. It was continually

GETTING WARMER,

as I progressed southward. At London I had received information that I must by no means go to Rome before October, as I might not be able to endure the intense heat of summer in central Italy.

The tourist must not always believe all that is said. Though it is not so pleasant to visit Rome in July or August, as later in the season, still it is quite as safe, if one takes the necessary precautions against fever. No one should eat much meat in Italy and Egypt. I lived upon milk, bread and fruit principally, and dressed in flannel; and as a consequence, never experienced much inconvenience from any source—not from heat even. At Rome I used an umbrella during the middle of the day, and in Egypt all of the day, but with that to protect me from the effect of the direct rays of the sun, I could get along tolerably well.

At Milan a young friend had cautioned me to be careful at Rome, as persons were often murdered there in broad daylight! I was not at all alarmed by that remark, because I had previously received similarly reports in regard to the morality of other cities, and had discovered that they were unfounded. As our train was sweeping on toward Rome, I apprehended little danger, therefore, from these sources, and after having formed the acquaintance of a certain Frenchman, the professor of mathematics of the University of Brest, who could speak a very little English, I began to have brighter hopes in regard to my visit to Rome.

CHAPTER XVIII.

ROME.

The sun set soon after we had passed Orbetello, and the moon rose about the same time. We had still two hours to Civita Vecchia and four hours to Rome, but I shall never forget the happiness and emotional excitement that prevailed among our passengers, as we were approaching the city of the Cæsars and of the Popes, on that pleasant moonlight evening. The light of the full moon cast a charm about every scene, and as we watched the appearance of tropical species of plants and trees under the subdued and enchanted light of the moon and stars, we felt that we were about to enter the celestial city under eminently fascinating circumstances. At 10:00 o'clock we were intently looking from the windows, each for the first glimpse of Rome. Will we reach the Tiber soon? As our train leaped upon the bridge and my French companion first saw the glassy surface of the historic stream, he, half distracted by solemnity of the occasion, exclaimed with a forced but feeble effort, "THE TIBER, *the Tiber!*" None was his own, and the enraptured Professor, sinking from the effects of an ecstatic swoon, grasped hold of me and with labored enunciation spoke in a low voice, saying, "I feel in–ex–pres–si–ble e–mo–sions!"

At 10:20 we entered the shed of the great Railway Station. It was my good fortune to meet a German porter who conducted me and my new companion to an excellent hotel (Albergo Torino E Trattoria duetto da Abrate—Via Principe Amedo in prossimita alla Stazione) where we took rooms together.

One sees a thousand strange and curious things at Rome that my limited space will preclude me from describing or mentioning, even. The gable-end of the Stazione (Station) has in base relief a representation of the traditional she-wolf nursing the twin brothers, Romulus and Remus, the founders of Rome.

Emblems unique and obscure in design, may be seen in almost every street. I saw in one place the hands of a clock dial in the form of snakes.

I did more justice to my eyes than to my feet, during my first day in Rome. The Column of Marcus Aurelius, the Post-Office, Castello S. Angelo, St. Peter, the Vatican, the Colosseum (*Amfiteatro Flavia*, or *Coliseo*) and the fountains, arches and ruins of ancient heathen temples that I passed on my way, gave me a pretty good practical idea of the Rome that I had read about in the books. Only the approaching darkness and the dread of walking alone through the suburbs of Rome under cover of night, could induce me on the evening of the first day to tear myself away from the crumbling heaps of stones which constitute the ruins of ancient Rome, so charming and grand to behold.

It required about three days of close study before I could readily identify on my map of ancient Rome, the temples of Vespasian, of Saturn, of Castor and Pollux, of Julius Cæsar, of Faustina, and of Venus and Roma; the triumphal arches of Titus, of Severus and of Constantine; the *Meta Sudante*, and the Column of Phocas, in the *Roman Forum;* also the Column of Trajan and other objects in the Forum of Trajan, and numerous other ruins of ancient Rome, including the aqueducts, baths, and the little round Temple of Vesta (?) on the left bank of the Tiber.

The Rome of to-day is about a mile and a half square, and has a population of 245,000 inhabitants. Ancient Rome occupied much more territory, and its population was *at the beginning of the 2nd century* about 1½ million. The ruins of ancient Rome cover a desolate area of several square miles in extent, besides what is covered by the modern city. Its walls are 15 miles in circuit.

Whatever may be said of the 364 churches of Rome, (including seven called Basilicae, namely: St. Peter, St. John Lateran, Santa Maria Maggiore, and Santa Croce in Gerusalemme, within the city, and St. Paolo, San Lorenzo and San Sebastian, outside of the walls), all agree, that

THE COLOSSEUM

is the *elephant* among the ruins of the old city. This stupendous structure is eliptical in form, measuring 615 feet through the longer diameter and 510 feet through the shorter, covering more than 5½ acres of ground. In the height of its glory 87,000 spectators could be accommodated within its walls! It is 156 feet high, but has no roof. The sailors of the imperial fleet used to stretch sail-cloth over it to exclude the burning rays of the sun. The arena is 279 feet by 174 feet. This building was begun in A. D. 72, and dedicated by Titus in A. D. 80. It was inaugurated by gladiatorial combats which lasted 100 days, during which time 5,000 wild animals were killed. About one third of the building is still preserved, and presents a scene to the beholder of overawing magnificence and grandeur. When I walked into the Cathedral of Milan, I felt as if its elevated ceiling was about to lift me up, but, standing in the arena of this vast amphitheater, one feels as if its stupendous walls would crush him to the ground. Close by the Colosseum is the Meta Sudans, and the Arch of Constantine which spans the *Via Triumphalis* and unites it with *Via Sacra* (the Sacred Way). This arch has three passages and is adorned with admirable sculptures. It was erected in 311, when Constantine declared himself in favor of Christianity. Following the Sacred way, toward the north, we first come to the arch of Titus and afterwards to

THE ROMAN FORUM.

The Sacred Way, it seems, was about ⅜ of a mile in length and extended from the Arch of Constantine or the northern end of the Colosseum near by, to the Capitol. Near the Capitol stands the Triumphal Arch of Septimius Severus, 75 feet high and 82 feet wide, with three passages. It was erected in honor of that emperor and his two sons Caracalla and Geta in A. D. 203, to commemorate victories. It was once surmounted by a brazen chariot with six horses, on which stood Severus, crowned by Victory. The pavement of the Forum, which has been laid bare by recent diggings, lies some twenty feet lower than the level of the street which now passes at the side of the diggings. Near the northern end stands the Column of Phocas, 54 feet high, which was erected in 608 in honor of the tyrant Phocas, of the Eastern Empire. All around the Forum stand what remains of the ancient temples, once dedicated to the deities which it was believed presided over the destinies of Rome, before the advent of Christianity. The broken pillars of ruined temples are seen on every side.

THE TABULARIUM.

The only relics still extant of the ancient Capitol of Rome are the ruins of the Tabularium, erected B. C. 78, by the consul Q. Lutatius Catulus for the reception of the state archives. The modern Capitol covers a part of it. The Tarpeian Rock, from which the condemned used to be thrown by the ancient Romans, is close by this edifice, *if* the *Rupe Tarpeia* still pointed out is the veritable one.

Adjoining the Tabularium is the *Schola Xantha*,

"With the *Colonnade of the Twelve Gods*, whose images Vettius Agorius Prætextatus, the præfectus urbi, and one of the principal champions of expiring paganism, erected here in A. D. 367." The *Twelve Gods* stand in base relief, on a beautiful vase in the corridor of the Capitoline Museum, in the following order: Jupiter, Juno, Minerva, Hercules, Apollo, Diana, Mars, Venus, Vesta, Mercury, Neptune and Vulcan. It is a remarkable coincidence (?), that there are: First, *Twelve* Lunations in a year; Second, *Twelve* Months in a year; Third, *Twelve* Constellations in the heavens; Fourth, *Twelve* Gods in the ancient mythology; Fifth, *Twelve* Labors of Hercules; Sixth, see Law of the *Twelve* tables (?), Encyclopædia Britannica on Burying; Seventh, *Twelve* Sons of Jacob; Eighth, *Twelve* Tribes of Israel; Ninth, *Twelve* Apostles of Christ; Tenth, *Twelve* Virtues and *Twelve* Vices represented in base reliefs in Notre Dame, Paris; Eleventh, *Twelve* Colossal statues facing the tomb of Napoleon I.; and Twelfth, *Twelve* units in a dozen.

It is strange enough that there are *a dozen dozen* of these curious *dozens!*

Did Pythagoras not also have twelve spheres to make his sphere-music?

Between the Tabularium and the Forum, about 150 feet southeast from the former, and near the Arch of Severus, are "the remains of

THE ROSTRA,

or orator's tribune, a name derived from the iron

prows of the war-ships of Antium with which the tribune was adorned after the capture of that town in B. C. 338. At the end of it was the *Umbilicus urbis Romæ*, or ideal center of the city and empire, the remains of which are recognizable. At the other end, below the street, are a few traces of the *Miliareum Aureum*, or central mile-stone of the roads radiating from Rome, erected by Augustus in B. C. 28. It is however doubtful whether these names are correctly applied to these remains."

THE TEMPLE OF CÆSAR

is situated on the east side of the Forum, with its front toward the Capitol. To this, "Caesar, in addition to other alterations made by him, transferred the tribune of the orators. This was now named the *Rostra Julia*, and from it, on the occasion of the funeral of the murdered dictator on the 19th or 20th March, B. C. 44, Mark Antony pronounced the celebrated oration which wrought so wonderfully on the passions of the excited populace. A funeral pyre was hastily improvised, and the unparalleled honor accorded to the illustrious dead of being burned in view of the most sacred shrines of the city. A column with the inscription 'parenti patriae' was afterwards erected here to commemorate the event. At a later period Augustus erected this temple in honor of 'Divus Julius,' his defied uncle and adopted father, and dedicated it to him in B. C. 29, after the battle of Actium. At the same time he adorned the rostra with prows of the captured Egyptian vessels."—*Bædeker.*

THE BATHS OF CARACALLA.

As an example of the magnificence of the ancient Roman baths, we may take the Thermae of Caracalla which could accommodate 1,600 bathers at a time! This establishment, now the largest mass of ruins in Rome, except the Colosseum, was 720 feet long and 372 feet wide. A flight of 98 steps lead to the roof which (the roof) has now tumbled down. This structure covered over six acres of ground, and had its porticoes, race course, &c., surrounded by a wall. The total area of the grounds is nearly 27 acres!

The Baths of Diocletian, erected in the 4th century, were 6,000 feet in perimeter and its number of daily bathers were 3,000.

THE PYRAMID OF CESTIUS.

"The Egyptian pyramidal form was not unfrequently employed by the Romans in the construction of their tombs." That of Cestius, who died within the last thirty years before Christ, is 116 feet high and 98 feet square at the base. It is constructed with bricks and covered with marble blocks.

Upon the Cemetery of St. Lorenzo, "the great modern burial-ground of Rome," I saw one or several small monuments or head stones which were in the form of pyramids. Here, as in Catholic burial-grounds generally in Europe, crosses take the place of memorial stones, except some of the latest interments are marked by marble slabs and monuments.

THE CATACOMBS,

or underground burial-places of Rome, are not quite as interesting as many suppose who have read large chapters and heard long addresses upon the subject. The passages are almost innumerable, intersecting each other in every direction and ranging in some places many stories above each other, but still, as you pass along in the dim light of a little taper, it appears much like a subterranean stone-quarry containing pigeon-holes for the dead.

THE TEMPLE OF VESTA.

The little round temple referred to on page 244, was once supposed to have been the temple of Vesta, but it is now quite certain that this was a mistake. It is 50 feet in diameter and each of its 20 Corinthian columns which constitute the circular colonnade around it, is 32 feet high. Wherever the Temple of Vesta may have stood, it is evident that from its eternal fires was borrowed the custom, still extant in Catholic churches, of keeping up a perpetual flame by means of tapers. Six Vestal Virgins sworn to perpetual virginity, used to watch the sacred flame upon the altar in the Temple of Vesta, and it is an impressive sight to see the same sacred and eternal flame still burning around the High Altar in St. Peter's. From what may still be seen in Europe in general, and at Rome in particular, it is evident that all or nearly all of the emblems, forms and ceremonies of the *early* Catholic Church were borrowed from ancient mythology.

OBELISKS AND FOUNTAINS.

The many magnificent fountains of Rome are all adorned with groups representing characters of ancient mythology, as is the case with nearly all the fountains of Europe and America, even unto this day, and the half a dozen or more obelisks of Rome are likewise monuments of the heathen origin of modern civilization. These, it seems, were first erected and dedicated to the sun, as we may infer from the fact that globes representing the sun surmount them. Since the introduction of the Christian religion, a figure of St. Peter with the cross is placed upon some of them. Hence, the development of religious ideas stands chronologically thus: First, Sun-worship and afterwards the elevation of St. Peter, and of the Cross. Judging from what we see on ancient monuments and in the churches, it is perhaps a fair question, whether St. Peter, the Virgin and other saints were not at one time quite as much the object of worship, as Christ himself?

ST. PETER'S.

"St. Peter's stands on the site of the circus of Nero, where many Christians were martyred and where St. Peter is said to have been buried after his crucifixion." An oratory (chapel?) stood here as early as A. D. 90. In 309 a basilica, half the size of what St. Peter's now is, was begun by Constantine. It was the grandest church of that time. "The crypt is now the only remnant of this early basilica." The building of the present edifice was commenced in 1506 by Julius II. Michael Angelo worked 17 years at it (to 1564). It was completed and "consecrated by Pope Urban VIII., on 18th November, 1626, on the 1300th anniversary of the day on which St. Silvester is said to have consecrated the original edifice."

This church contains 29 altars, besides the high altar. "Its area is 212,321 sq. ft., while that of the cathedral of Milan is 117,678, St. Paul's at London 108,982, St. Sophia at Constantinople 96,497, and the Cathedral of Cologne 73,903 sq. ft." The nave is 87 feet wide and 150 feet high, and the dome is 138 feet in diameter (5 feet less than that of the Pantheon) and some 450 feet high. One might fill a volume in describing its rich marble pavement, its 148 massive columns, its gilded chapels and ceiling, its fine sculpture, and the thousand and one objects in and about it that render it the most imposing as well as the largest church in the world. Imagine yourself in the middle of a church occupying over five acres, whose High Altar stands under a brass canopy 95 feet high, and weighing 93 tons, and whose *Confessio* is surrounded by 89 burning lamps! The total cost of the edifice is about $85,000,000. [It should always be remembered that labor has been twice to three times as cheap in Europe as it is now in this country]. "The expense of erecting this church was so heavy that Julius II. and Leo X. resorted to the sale of indulgences to raise the money, and this lead to the Reformation."

THE LATERAN

is the church of the Pope as bishop of Rome, and here his coronation takes place. "It takes the precedence even of St. Peter, in ecclesiastical rank, being, as the inscription on its facade sets forth, '*Ominum Urbis Et Urbis Ecclesiarum Mater Et Caput.*'"

If St. Peter's had not the advantage of a piazza that is unrivaled in magnificence, I think the lofty facade of the Lateran would present a view of more imposing grandeur, even, than that stately structure. The interior of this church is very beautiful. It must not be supposed that St. Peter's has no rivals in beauty. Even in Rome it does not seem to stand alone. Of the 363 other churches in the great city of churches, there are numbers that vie with it in the beauty and perfection of some particular portions.

SANTA MARIA MAGGIORE.

"The Virgin appeared simultaneously to the devout Roman patrician Johannes and to Pope Liberius in their dreams, commanding them to erect a church to her on the spot where they should find a deposit of snow on the following morning (August 5th)." The Basilica Liberiana which was erected in obedience of this vision, was succeeded by a church named S. Maria Mater Dei (A. D. 432) and later by the present edifice. Almost every church in Rome has its legend. I have seen no other church that seemed so rich in gold, precious alabaster and many other kinds of beautiful and costly stones. Its panelled roof is gilt with the first gold brought to Spain from South America, and presented to the Pope by Ferdinand and Isabella.

Near S. Maria Maggiore is the church of

S. ANTONIO ABBATE,

to which are brought the horses, mules, cows, &c., during the week following the feast of the saint (January 17–23). On the 23rd, the Pope and many persons of the higher classes send their horses here to be blessed and sprinkled with holy water.

THE SCALA SANTA

referred to on page 189 of this book, are in a church near the Lateran. They were brought to Rome by the Empress Helena and may only be ascended on the knees. They are partly covered with boards to save the stones from being worn away by the thousands that ascend it. Two adjoining stairways are for the descent.

S. PIETRO IN VINCOLI

was founded about 442, as the receptacle for the chains of St. Peter, which had been presented by Eudoxia, wife of Valentinian III., to Pope Leo I. This church contains the famous statue of Moses with horns, by Michael Angelo. Mediaeval Christian artists generally represented Moses with horns, owing to an erroneous translation of Exodus XXXIV., 35. Michael Angelo represented these horns upon the head of Moses as having been about three inches in length.

S. MARIA IN ARACŒLI

probably occupies the site of the Temple of Jupiter. Its present altar encloses an ancient altar which is said to have been erected by Augustus. "According to a legend of the 12th century, this was the spot where the Sibyl Tibur appeared to the emperor, whom the senate proposed to elevate to the rank of a god, and revealed to him a vision of the Virgin and her Son."

This church is approached by a very high flight of steps rising from the foot of those leading to the piazza of the modern Capitol, and "the interior is vast, solemn, and highly picturesque. It was here, as Gibbon tells us, that on the 15th of October, 1764, as he sat musing amidst the ruins of the Capitol, while the barefooted friars were singing vespers, the idea of writing the 'Decline and Fall' of the city first started to his mind."

THE VATICAN

has been the residence of the Popes since their return from Avignon in France, where they had resided from 1309 to 1377. It is now the most extensive palace in the world, being three stories high and 1,151 feet long by 767 feet wide, covering over 20 acres! The palace comprises 20 courts, eight grand staircases and two hundred smaller ones, and is said to contain 11,000 halls, chapels, saloons and private apartments. Since the Italian occupation, Pope Pius IX. considers himself a prisoner in his own palace, though strange to say, there are no doors locked except those which he locks himself on the inside! King Victor Emanuel, though excommunicated by the Pope in the most indecent language that ever fell from human lips, has done no violence to the person of the Pope, and now contents himself as an outsider of the church.

The masses can now no longer "go to Rome to see the Pope," for he neither ventures forth from his palace into the city for exercise and pleasure, as he used to, neither does he hold any public receptions. My French companion who had come to Rome for the purpose of making a present of several hundred dollars to the Pope, insisted on my accompanying him, as he was allowed a private interview, but I could not avail myself of the opportunity.

The galleries and museums of the palace are the richest in the world, in Roman and Christian antiquities. Here are the paintings which have rendered Raphael and Angelo immortal to fame. They are almost innumerable. These masters translated the Bible into pictures, and here are the originals of many of the cuts that adorn our finely illustrated family Bibles. Michael Angelo painted 22 months (1508–11) at the ceiling of the Sixtine

Chapel. In the Loggie, Raphael represents God in the person of an old man wearing a long gray beard and attired in the oriental costume.

MUSEUMS.

The principal museums in Rome are the Christian and the Gregorianum Lateranense in the Lateran; the Etruscan, the Egyptian and the Museum of Christian Antiquities in the Vatican; and the Capitoline Museum, on Capitoline Hill. The vast stores of ancient art contained in these, brings the beholder back again to the strange scenes of the distant past, as do perhaps no other museums in the world. To do justice to these collections would require many weeks, and a mere catalogue of their contents would cover many pages. Among the most interesting apartments of the Capitoline Museum, are the Room of the Dying Gladiator, the Room of the Philosophers, the Room of the Busts of the Emperors, the Room of Venus, &c. Bædeker guides the tourist through Rome by means of 312 pages of description in fine print. It may be proper to observe here, that Murray leads the visitor in the same way through London by means of a guide-book of 316 pages, and Galignani has 438 pages on Paris, exclusive of the tables of contents.

In regard to the brilliant and magnificent churches of Italy, which, for beauty, throw those of the rest of the world into the shade, I will here add that their overawing grandeur assisted materially in making man a humble and submissive being; and possibly taught him to take the first steps from ancient barbarity toward civilization and refinement.

Several square miles of ancient Rome lying in ruins, is now unoccupied, and many of the roads which intersect this desolate area are lined on both sides by walls from 7 to 10 or 12 feet in height. They are plastered white and overgrown by the ivy; and as one walks along in these, he may well occupy his time in watching a species of little reptiles that are very nimble but shy, running up the high smooth walls as easily as along the ground. They are harmless, no doubt, but I dreaded them quite as much as if I had been in a similar danger of treading upon snakes! They dart like arrows across the streets, and in their reckless haste of attempting to cross the street to avoid me, they frequently came near losing their lives under my feet! They are about 3 to 6 inches long, we will say; have four legs as near as I could count, and are very slim, resembling the snake in form and the frog in features. Good-by, Old Rome!

I spent 8 days in London, 17 in Paris and 6 in Rome; doing to one city about as much justice as to the other, in those various periods of time; but if one would come to Rome first, he would not be able to tear himself away in less than a few weeks. No one should travel any other way than *against* the course of civilization, on his first visit to Europe.

In my course from Liverpool to Rome I enjoyed new sights in a constant flow, like that of a steady rain. I do not believe that it would be well for an American to be abruptly transported to Rome and awake one morning there. The strange sights would assail him suddenly, like a flood of angry waters!

CHAPTER XIX.

ROME TO BRINDISI.

From Rome I went to Pompeii, stopping long enough at Naples, however, to learn that the impudence of the pestiferous porters is quite unendurable. Italy throughout is much infested with porters, but in the southern section of the peninsula they are a regular pest, which at times becomes epidemic. During the traveling season it seems as if everybody was a porter. Sometimes they will surround the traveler and assail him on every side, asking him to let them carry his baggage. Sometimes I found them to be of great service in finding hotels for me, but at other times I was much inconvenienced by their attacks. I think it was at Naples, where a dozen or more of them yelled at me all at the same time, each desirous of carrying my satchel. As none of them could speak in a language that I understood, I declined to let any one have it. Each one evinced his earnestness by taking hold of my baggage while asking for it. After taking turns at their chances in this way for a while, at the same time crowding the path in front of me so that I could not proceed, one of them in his greediness almost tore my satchel out of my hands, I responded to his supplication with such a tremendous *no*, that the next fellow assumed a stooping posture and asked me in a whisper! These people deserve our pity rather than censure. Many of them are evidently sometimes in a famishing condition. But few who have not seen, can form an idea of the poverty which reigns in some sections of Southern Italy, especially between Naples and Brindisi. I saw children running about in this section, that had little of clothing save a shirt, which was generally torn in every part; some few, below the age of about six or eight years, had not even a thread of clothing upon their bodies. An elderly man that was plowing with a pair of oxen, as is the custom in Italy, was accompanied by his wife who was well dressed, but he wore only a shirt that reached to his knees, and a hat. I spent a Sunday at Brindisi, and observed that people keep no Sunday there. All the people wear old and tattered garments, and I could not see a hat, a coat or a pair of pantaloons on the person of one of the hundreds that thronged the market-place all Sunday, that looked as if it had been new at any time within the last few years!

The railroad tunnels are even more numerous than in the Black Forest. In some places it becomes impossible to read in the cars, as the train is much of the time under the mountains. From the window of the cars I saw a man with his bare feet in a tub treading grapes, for the purpose of making wine. It reminded me of the way, as it is said, some made their sourcrout in this country some forty-five or fifty years ago.

I spent a day among the ruins of Pompeii and in the ascent of Mount Vesuvius. Pompeii was a town of about 30,000 inhabitants when it was destroyed by an eruption of old Vesuvius in A. D. 79. On the 24th of August a dense shower of ashes covered the town 3 feet in thickness, but allowed the inhabitants time to escape. Only of those which returned to recover valuables, &c., were overtaken and covered by the shower of red hot rapilli, or fragments of pumice-stone, which, with succeeding showers of ashes, covered the town to the depth of 7–8 feet. "The present superincumbent mass is about 20 feet in thickness." In the one third of the town already excavated the skeletons of some 500 have been found. Casts of bodies found in 1863, were made by pouring plaster of Paris into the cavities where they had lain, and the figures of the deceased in their death-struggle are thus obtained. Bædeker devotes 25 pages to a description of the wonders and curiosities of this exhumed town.

The ascent of Vesuvius required about six hours. We started at 6:30 in the morning and returned at 12:30 p. m. The distance from Pompeii, which stands at its foot, to the top of it is about 5 miles in a straight line, and eight miles by the paths. Mules can ascend half-way; but I took a guide and walked the whole distance. At the point where the mules must be abandoned, a number of guides offered to carry me up, or to drag me up by means of a rope! But I climbed it. A cloud hangs over it all the time, which is occasioned by the column of steam that issues from its crater. The entire upper part of the peak is perfectly bare of vegetation, and covered with fine cinders, rapilli, &c., through which escapes a gas that almost suffocates the ascending traveler. At the top we shouted into the crater and heard distinct echos after two seconds, which proves that the mouth of the crater reflected the sound at the depth of about 1,000 or 1,100 feet!

From Pompeii I returned to Naples and spent the night there. Early on Thursday morning I went to the "Stazione" (Station) and left for Brindisi. The temperature was 90 degrees in the shade, in the afternoon. Some people have constructed artificial caves which they use as stables, for their cattle; and possibly some have such rude grottos for their homes!

CHAPTER XX.

ON THE MEDITERRANEAN.

On Monday morning, September 26th, at 4:00 o'clock a. m., I stepped on board the steamship "Avoca" to take passage for Alexandria. Brindisi, like Havre, is one of the finest places in the world to leave! Almost everything about it is repulsive. I saw many children there that have possibly never seen a washing day in their lives! I sailed for Egypt with great reluctance, for I had already my misgivings about the property of tourists from civilized nations going thither for sight-seeing. Well one does see sights there—but, *such sights!*

Our voyage to Egypt was a very prosperous and, I may say, a pleasant one. Time, some eighty hours. As first and second class passage is unreasonably high, boarding costing $9–$10 per day, I took third class passage, and with a special outlay of a few dollars obtained acceptable meals. The steamer belonged to an English line, and it was one of the most pleasant incidents of my entire tour, to hear a company of sailors chime in one evening and sing "Kiss Me Mother, Kiss Your Darling." I had heard little English speaking for months, and now to hear that old familiar tune, five thousand miles away from home, made me feel as if America could after all not be so very far off! There were no storms, nor was their any cool night air upon that "summer seat." I slept one night on deck, without even an awning of canvass over me,—how pleasant it was at night to awake and see the winter constellation of Orion as high up already in September, as I was wont to see it in America in the month of January! We reached

ALEXANDRIA

on the fourth day after leaving the coasts of Italy. Perhaps I can not give the reader a better idea of what a blank Egypt seems to one who has luxuriated for months amid the scenes of Europe, than by leaving my chapter on Egypt a blank one. A great deal too much has been written about Egypt and the East, already. What profitable example can we take from those semi-barbarians? A young man who was just returning from a tour through Egypt and Greece, had told me already at Rome, that "going to see the East is done mostly for the name of having done the thing." He had been disappointed, and so was I. Why do tourists speak so much about the pyramids, after returning from Egypt? Because there is little else to be seen there or to talk about! And these are not half the wonders that many imagine who falsely presume that the building of the entire structures were undertaken at once. The broad foundation of 13 acres, which constitutes the base of the greatest, was not undertaken at one time; but only a small pyramid was at first reared, and around this, as a nucleus, was built layer after layer, until the structure assumed the amazing proportions which now characterize the astounding magnificence of the great pyramids on the plains of Geezeh. Thus at whatever time the sovereign might die, his pyramid would be almost complete, and would be large or small, in proportion to the time spent upon it. Perhaps succeeding generations built at some of the larger pyramids. They are monuments erected to the memory of kings or ruling families, and contain their tombs. Such, at least, is a plausible solution of the problem of pyramid-building.

CAIRO.

At Cairo I engaged a guide whom I paid three dollars for accompanying me as many hours, and bargained with him that he must furnish the mules, (or donkeys I should have said), and pay all the contingent expenses. We visited the Mosk of Mohamet Ali in the Citadel, the Mosk of Hassen and others. Attendants at the doors provided us with slippers, for no one is allowed to tread the fine carpet (or matting?) of these holy temples with his shoes. Hats must be kept on, however. A large mosque generally consists of porticoes surrounded a square open court, containing a fountain or tank in the center. Here every Mussulman washes his hands and feet before he goes to prayers. They sometimes would here bathe their whole bodies in former times! It is not at all surprising that washing of feet should have become a part of the religious ceremonies in countries like Egypt, where washing is quite as necessary to existence, as eating and drinking, even. I wish they had pure water enough to wash themselves a dozen times a day. They would certainly be, what we consider very dirty, more than half the time, even then. As it is, they must take their untanned goat-skin bags and collect the luke-warm water which they find in dirty pools, and take it home for drinking purposes! It is impossible for the poor Egyptians to keep themselves clean. It rains only about three days in a year, and the wind takes so much dust into the air that one can often neither see or breath for a few seconds. This dust collected in such a thick layer upon my body, the first day, that I could in the evening plow furrows with my fingers upon any portion of my skin. I protected my eyes, by hiding my face in my shawl, during the most dangerous busts; but being ignorant of the necessity of putting cotton into my ears, I lost the hearing of one of them, which I only recovered quite lately. Hundreds of people in Cairo are blind, and certainly the majority of them have but poor sight or have very sore eyes! What wretched houses they live in! Many of the huts in their villages consist of but a single apartment, large enough for a person to lie down lengthwise in it, but not more than 5 feet wide. The walls and roof are all mud, and so low that a man cannot stand erect in some of them! These mud-huts have no doors even! The men as well as the women wear long flowing garments, like those represented in our picture Bibles. Many of the poor women have but a single garment to cover their bodies with. This consists of a hood-like covering for the head, and a loose flowing robe, all in one piece; having neither shoes nor the other garments to make themselves presentable in any decent or refined society. Many present pictures of indescribable wretchedness. I saw a woman nurse her child in the cars, who, when presented with an apple for her babe, returned her thanks *without a smile*, even, to the giver! These people are in too great misery to know what it is to feel happy! I saw men and women speak by the hour in the train without once turning into any pleasant mood. How my pity might have turned into joy, could I only have seen them indulge in a hearty laugh occasionally! Some of their girls and women of all ages will still ride the donkey, after the oriental style. The middle and poorer classes of Egyptians will eat little snails and fish fried with the heads, scales and all the appurtenances of their internal structures! In the East they churn the butter in bags made of untanned goat-skins, having the hair inside. Moreover, they bring the butter upon the table without doing so much as to comb it, even!

When I had seen these things, and was informed that on account of the cholera which was still raging in Syria, the surrounding nations had interposed a quarantine, so that if I would venture to go on to Joppa (which I could have reached in a few hours), I would become a prisoner, I soon decided that I would rather not see a people (the Syrians) that is more miserable than the Egyptians, even, than be in danger of being obliged to partake of food that could scarcely have failed to make me sick. Crossing the desert by rail, meeting large caravans of camels, and seeing the palm-trees, the minarets, the mosks, the pyramids, the muddy waters of the Nile, and above all the curious styles of the oriental costume, are interesting enough to one that comes to Egypt with ordinary expectations and correct information in regard to the country; but I did not expect to find the Egyptians a black inferior race, that would fight with each other on the pavements in the largest cities in broad day-light, violently tear my property out of my hands in sight of the finest square in Alexandria, carry naked children upon their shoulders in their large towns, and seat themselves around large dishes of rice and gravy mixing the same with their fingers and conveying it to their mouths in the palms of their hands! Numbers of them will dine without the use of either knives, forks or spoons, and when dinner is over, there is but one dish to be washed. Each has two hands and ten fingers to clean, and washing those, ends the whole matter! These are extreme cases, of course. Some live decently, too. Some *few* of the ruling classes, in luxury, perhaps. From Cairo I traveled by rail to Ismalia, thence by the Suez Canal to Port Said, where I spent the Sunday (October 3rd). On Tuesday I reached Alexandria again. I there put up at a first-class hotel (for travelers from civilized and refined nations can not enjoy themselves at inferior hotels in Egypt), and stayed five days, until the next steamer sailed for Brindisi. The hotel contained an excellent cafe, where ten intelligent and refined ladies and four gentlemen, all natives of Austria, were engaged to render music every evening for a whole year. One evening as I sat in the cafe at my supper, a poor boy came in to sell flowers; for what we must pay in this country for a drink, I bought a bouquet almost as large as a bucket, and when the next lady came to collect for the music, I gave her the bouquet as a present to the whole company. It was worth more than an introduction to the entire party, and for the balance of my stay I was always well entertained, and was kindly informed of anytning that I asked in regard to the manners and customs of oriental life. The people of every nation under the sun, travel in Egypt in the habits of their own peculiar national costumes—the Turk with his turban, the Greek with his red cap, and the Arabians, East Indians, Russians, and all the nations of Western Europe are represented here, all wearing their own peculiar styles and fashions. The money too is a mixture of the coins of a dozen different countries. None except the poorest women will come out of their houses without having their faces covered with thick black veils.

ON THE "HOME-STRETCH."

I do not know where I was the happiest, when I reached the coasts of Italy and saw dear Europe again, when I reached Paris, or when I landed at New York and was finally again ushered into the sweet scenes of home! But I remember well that I left no city with so much regret as Paris. How I watched to see the last glimmering rays of its ten thousand gas-jets, as our train moved away at the silent midnight hour of October 22nd.

I had stopped at Milan to see the grand peagent of Emperor William of Germany, and King Victor Emanuel of Italy, with a retinue of some 22,000 militia, with which they held a military drill, and saw the illumination of the Cathedral on that memorable occasion; besides I had stopped a day at Rome, and two at Paris; yet I made my return trip from Alexandria to New York in 25 days, sleeping but 7 nights in comfortable beds in all that time. Sleeping in the cars and on the ships, never amounted to much. I made this haste on account of the now rapidly approaching winter.

CONCLUSION.

Notwithstanding the influence which the church and the political powers of Rome, in earlier times, and which Paris and the spirit of progress in later years, have exerted to the contrary, the manners, customs and institutions of the people are still so different that the people of the Western Continent can not form correct ideas of European life without having first visited portions of it. For want of a standard of comparison, the reader is often utterly deceived by fine poetical descriptions, because he can not properly construe the language.

A tour of ordinary length and duration can now be made through the western nations of Europe, with less expense than is generally believed, as may be inferred from the fact that my entire tour of nearly fourteen thousand miles, cost less than seven hundred dollars. Many travelers lose forty per cent. of their money by imposition, and others are more careless and extravagant than they ought. If I could not have spoken German, it would have cost me several hundred dollars more. Could I have spoken French, it might have cost me a hundred dollars less. The expenses of making the tour of England, France and Switzerland are from $300 to $1,000, according to the style in which one wishes to travel; but a young man who wishes to spent $1,000 in educating himself, will make the best investment by spending half of it in traveling in foreign lands. He will there lay such a sure foundation for a correct knowledge of the institutions of the world, as no amount of reading can ever afford him. Let the enterprising "go west," but the student should see eastern countries.

THE END.

www.ingramcontent.com/pod-product-compliance
Lightning Source LLC
LaVergne TN
LVHW010236110826
845151LV00004B/1312

9781425524876